AN EARLY BREAKFAST

MIKE JENKIN

ISBN: 978-1-925590-72-2
Published by Vivid Publishing
A division of Fontaine Publishing Group
P.O. Box 948, Fremantle
Western Australia 6959
www.vividpublishing.com.au

Cataloguing-in-Publication data is available from the National Library of Australia

ACKNOWLEDGEMENTS

I would like to acknowledge the assistance my son Matthew Jenkin provided with the preparation and editing of the manuscript. Without his help and encouragement this book would have never seen the light of day.

FOREWORD

This narrative is offered as a tribute to the thousands upon thousands of young men who, in the decade and a half following the end of the Second World War, gave two of the prime years of their lives to the service of their country — the British National Servicemen.

It is not a war story — there are no heroics; though it is true to say that the great majority of the NS men, willingly or not, acquitted themselves pretty well in their role as their nation's defenders. In the nature of things, there were many brave souls among them, more than a few of whom made the ultimate sacrifice. I leave the chronicling of their deeds to people better qualified for the task.

Rather, this is the catalogue of the experiences of one unre-markable member of the NS brotherhood — experiences that are fairly typical of those of a myriad of others.

Mike Jenkin
Baldivis 2010.

1

THE PRELIMINARIES

In the years following the end of the Second World War, Britain had enormous military commitments all over the world. In part these obligations related to her membership of various international organisations, such as the United Nations and the North Atlantic Treaty Organisation, and in part to the desire to retain control of her numerous colonies and territories (this was becoming increasingly difficult in the face of growing agitation for independence). Or it may have been the intention at least to delay the evil day until enough people could be trained to manage the complicated business of self-government, after a century or more of colonial rule and so to avoid the otherwise inevitable chaos that would ensue, following the premature handover of power.

And so it was that the Union Jack flew proudly over military establishments, naval bases and Royal Air Force stations in places as far-flung as Germany, The West Indies, Gibraltar, Malta, Cyprus, the Suez Canal Zone, Palestine, Aden, Kenya, Singapore, Malaya, Hong Kong, Japan and Korea, and probably a few other places as well. On top of all this, there was also a large standing army stationed in Britain itself, in garrisons scattered all over the country. There were of course hundreds of thousands, maybe millions of servicemen still in uniform, many of whom had served as conscripts for anything up to six years, in mostly uncomfortable, and very often dangerous situations. Since their release could not be delayed forever, it was clear that replacements would have to be found, and very soon at that. Obviously this was going to require the recruitment of a host of fit, healthy young men. It was realised very early in the piece that there were never going to be enough volunteers to meet these needs, so that a degree of compulsion would be required. It was only for these reasons that the institution of National Service came into being. In fact, this was not really such a radical idea, since it was simply and extension of the existing state of affairs, the only difference that the new recruits would be enlisted for a fixed term, rather than "for the duration". To begin with the term was set at eighteen months, but this period was later found to be inadequate, and was increased to two years, where it remained until the early sixties, when National Service was abolished. By that time Harold Macmillan's "winds of change" were blowing at gale force; and former colonies had for the most part achieved independence. Moreover the Cold War had thawed considerably, so that the threat from the Eastern Bloc was no longer the serious concern that it had formerly been. Relations between Russia and the West had improved immeasurably since the death of Stalin in 1953. These two factors combined which meant that the numbers of service personnel that were required to ensure national security gradually declined over the years. Pay and conditions in the services improved out of sight so it was then possible to induce enough volunteers to "take the King's Shilling".

In the late forties and early fifties however, things were not so rosy. Many of the wartime regulations and restrictions were still in effect as life slowly returned to normal. People were still required to carry on their person an Identity Card, which had to be shown on demand to a police officer, or any serviceman in uniform. Since this provision was hardly ever invoked however, it caused little inconvenience or resentment. Similarly the continuation of conscription was widely accepted as being a necessary precaution against any threat that might emerge. As far as those most affected, i.e. the youth of the country was concerned there was very little resistance to the prospect of being called up – after all we had been raised on a diet of Hollywood heroics, such as Errol Flynn almost single-handedly rescuing Burma from the horrors of the Yellow Peril, or John Wayne wreaking havoc upon the Japanese on Iwo Jima, or Audie Murphy collecting a couple of dozen decorations as he ended the careers of an estimated 240 German soldiers, not counting those he scared to death, on his way to "Hell and Back". (At least, the latter really had been a soldier, the film being based on actual events, of which he had been a part). With all this inspiring stuff in mind, a couple of years in Her Majesty's uniform didn't seem too bad a prospect after all.

The first step in the transition from civilian life to the military was the obligation on the part of the prospective conscript, as soon as possible after his eighteenth birthday, to register with the Ministry of Labour and National Service. This move resulted in the issue of another card, once again showing all the relevant details, and accompanied by instructions to stand by for further orders. This I did towards the end of February 1952, then carried on as normal to await the next development. About five months later, near the end of July, I received by mail a directive to present myself for medical examination at the Drill Hall in Redruth, the nearest recruitment centre to my home. When I arrived there I found about two dozen other young blokes already assembled, and looking about as bewildered as I felt. It soon transpired that they were a mixed bunch, coming from all walks of life, not really surprising since the National Service Act applied to everybody without exception. Some other countries, from time to time, employed a kind of quota system to fill their manpower needs – a sort of lottery, in which only the unfortunate fell victim. Not so in Britain, where the net was cast far and wide, and was of fine mesh, so that few indeed evaded its coils. There were, however provisions for the exemption of persons engaged in work considered to be of vital importance to the national wellbeing. Examples of such jobs were the mining industry, the Merchant Navy, the armaments industry, many farm workers who could show that they could not easily be replaced. These people, together with certain other categories, were not conscripted as long as they remained in those jobs, which were termed "reserved occupations." If however they left their job, and took up employment in an industry that was not reserved, they became liable for National Service at any time up until their twenty-sixth birthday, at which all such liability ceased.

There were two young fellows of my acquaintance who fell into this trap. The first, who was a few years older than I, had joined the Merchant Navy, intending at the time to make it his career. However, on one of his voyages to Australia, he became so distressed by the persistent amorous advances of the bo'sun that he jumped ship in Sydney and disappeared into the bush. There he took a job on a sheep station, where he remained for a couple of years until he became homesick, and returned home. Within a matter of a few weeks he was in an Army uniform, and spent the best part of the next two years in Egypt. The other one was the son of a local "gentleman farmer" who had set up operations on a farm not far from ours. He managed to convince the authorities that his son's help was indispensable, and so he secured exemption for him. All went well for a year or two, but then bad husbandry, the result of inexperience and over-expenditure on costly and largely unnecessary machinery and the like brought the enterprise to the brink of bankruptcy, and the farm had to be sold. The would – be farmer returned to his former occupation, whereupon his son, no longer enjoying the sanctuary of a reserved occupation , was conscripted forthwith , and spent a couple of uncomfortable years as a member of the Royal Air Force , serving in Aden.

Besides outright exemption, there was another opportunity at least to delay conscription, and that was to apply for deferment. This meant that provided you could show a valid reason, you could put off your enlistment for a specified period. This arrangement was designed particularly to accommodate trade apprentices, who would not normally complete their apprenticeship until they were 21 years of age. It was felt that it would be unnecessarily disruptive, and probably damaging to their future careers, to take them away from their training for two years and expect that they would be able to resume afterwards without considerable difficulty. So the authorities had a heart after all! This option was also open to those intending to undertake tertiary education, for example at a university or other institution, though there were very few people who availed themselves of the privilege, preferring instead to get their NS over with and return fresh to their studies afterwards. There were a very few people who evaded their obligations altogether by emigrating before they could be drafted, and remained overseas until they passed the age limit for conscription. They were then able to return to Britain, quite free of any commitments.

There was one other avenue of escape from the all-encompassing net, and that was to claim exemption on the grounds of religious or conscientious objection. It was by no means easy to prove that such a claim was genuine, and this difficulty, added to the fact that there was a general disdain, even contempt, among the public for what were termed "conchies". Only the truly committed therefore took this step, and in my opinion it took a great deal more courage to do so than to take the easy way, and betray one's principles.

A few years later I learned from a Norwegian friend that his country's government had devised a clever plan to deal with this problem. In Norway at the time they had universal conscription for eighteen months military service. Anyone who objected to service in the armed forces was given the option of joining a labour battalion instead. These battalions wore uniforms, and were organised in much the same way as military units, but did not bear arms, and engaged in public works programs such as road building and forest management and so forth. In order to discourage frivolous claims the term of enlistment in the labour battalions was for two years instead of eighteen months, so that only genuine cases would apply. This seemed to me to be an admirable solution to the problem, and I wondered why it was not adopted by other countries. Perhaps it was felt there might be objections from the trade unions (at the time the pay of the labour battalions being the same as soldiers, was considerably lower than civilian workers).

But back to the Drill Hall. When the last of the stragglers finally arrived, we were marshalled into some sort of orderly line and the business began. For the next hour or two we were subjected to the most thorough and meticulous medical examination I had ever experienced. As instructed, we stripped off and shuffled along as we were in turn poked, prodded, listened to with a stethoscope, required to cough while being grasped by our most sensitive parts. Teeth and ears were minutely scrutinized, and we were closely examined for any signs of what in those days were coyly known as "social diseases". This last indignity was routinely applied at intervals throughout the next two years, particularly in overseas postings, where, quite logically, such dangers were considered more likely to be encountered. In the field these inspections, called FFI's that is "free from infection", were performed by the most junior officer available, and for many of these poor fellows the task proved acutely embarrassing.

The last part of the medical was the eye test, and it was here that I received a surprise. One bloke, when asked to read the chart, rather shyly confessed that he couldn't read very well. It transpired that he was almost entirely illiterate, a most unusual situation in those days of free and compulsory education. Looking back, I suspect that he probably suffered from dyslexia, of which little was known at the time. Anyway, the Army was up to the challenge, and produced another chart, which depicted animals instead of letters. Being a country boy, the lad was able to identify these with no hesitation, proving that there was nothing wrong with his eye sight. At a guess, I would say that he probably ended up in the Pioneer Corps, where, since their main function was digging trenches and suchlike, the lack of literary skills would not be an issue.

When all the examinations had been completed, we were treated to a short address explaining in some detail that we were entering into a commitment of a serious nature, and that un-questioning loyalty and obedience would be expected of us. After filling in a form or two, and pledging allegiance to the Crown and so on, we were invited to state which branch of the Services we would prefer to join. An answer "None of them" would not be accepted! We were told that, as far as possible, our preferences would be honoured subject of course to the exigencies of the service. This turned out to be a fairly worthless promise, as the following examples will show. There were two brothers I knew, one of whom was a carpenter and the other an electrician. The carpenter naturally expected to join the Royal Engineers where his experience would obviously be useful. He was assigned to the Royal Artillery. The electrician, whose qualifications fitted him for a career in the Royal Electrical and Mechanical Engineers, ended up in the Duke of Cornwall's Light Infantry (DCLI, also known by some as The Dirty Duke's). I myself applied for the DCLI, of which I was very proud, not only because it was our County regiment, but also because an uncle by marriage had been a member of it in the First World War, serving with great distinction in what was then known as Mesopotamia, and elsewhere in the Middle East, and being awarded the Greek Military Cross for, as the citation read, "conspicuous courage and cheerfulness". I admired him very much of course, but to tell the truth my decision to choose the DCLI as my preference had less to do with the desire or ambition to emulate him, than with the fact that the DCLI home base was at Bodmin, only about twenty five miles from my home, it would mean that less of my leave time would be lost in travelling.

In any case, as Robbie Burns so sagely observed, "The best-laid plans of Mice and Men gang aft agley", or words to that effect, I ended up in the Royal Artillery. At first I was somewhat peeved at this development, but later on I was grateful to the Army, because it became evident to me that we gunners had an easier time of it than the footsloggers, or the P.B.I, as they were sometimes called (i.e. Poor Bloody Infantry). Much later on I worked out the reason for the Army's apparent bloody-mind-edness. I realised that there are three ways of doing things: there's the right way, and there's the wrong way, and then there's the Army way. Aware of this, the Army preferred to take raw material, as it were, for the specialised trades, so that they could be trained in the Army way, without any preconceived ideas of how things ought to be done. By this means two important objectives would be achieved. Firstly, a lot of unnecessary confusion would be averted, and secondly the instructor would be spared the possible embarrassment of having recruits in his class who knew more about the subject than he did himself.

Anyway, the medical and all the associated paperwork having been completed, we were now free to go home. Before we left, we were each given yet another card, this one showing the results of the examination, and the grade we had achieved. I, and probably most of the others, received a Grade I rating, which meant that we were considered fit enough to serve anywhere we were needed. These cards, incidentally, were a far cry from the plastic-fantastic, computerised marvels so familiar to us today, and without which life would scarcely be possible. Then the cards were simple little bits of cardboard, printed usually on both sides, with spaces for the official in charge to enter, in ink, the details of the bearer. Surprisingly, these were very durable- I still have mine to this day. The business of the day thus concluded, we departed for home, there to await the next development.

2

THE RECRUIT

The next development was not long in coming: in late August I received a bulky, official-looking envelope, no stamp just 'O.H.M.S.' containing detailed instructions to the effect that I was to report for duty on the sixteenth of September to the R.A. Training Regiment in Oswestry, which it appeared was somewhere in Shropshire. I was to travel by train to Oswestry station by a certain time, and to wait there for the Army truck that would take me to the camp. For my convenience, and no doubt to forestall any possible excuse on my part for failure to comply on the grounds of financial hardship preventing me from buying a railway ticket, included was a railway voucher entitling me to a one-way, third-class journey from Perranporth to Oswestry. So there was no way out! Not that I was looking for a way out in any case- on the contrary, I was rather looking forward what would undoubtedly be a new experience. In any case, default was never a realistic option, since a failure to show up without a very good reason would result, in a very short time, in a couple of burly Military Policemen appearing at our door, to the titillation of nosy neighbours, and the acute embarrassment of the family. Unthinkable!

The instructions were to travel light: all that was required was my person, and whatever items of toiletry that might be deemed necessary. Every other necessity would be provided at Her

Majesty's expense. So, on the appointed day, I boarded the train with my bag of goodies, containing toothbrush, razor, and a few sandwiches for the journey, and set off for the station in a fairly cheerful frame of mind. There were a few misgivings of course; I was at this time rather immature, and had never been far from home before. All in all though, I was confident that I could manage whatever was to come, and comforted by the thought that I would not be alone. There would be plenty of others in the same boat! The journey was long and somewhat tedious at times, but I got much enjoyment from admiring the ever-changing, and often beautiful scenery. That, together a chat now and then with my fellow passengers, some of whom were interested when they learned that I was going to join up, and asked many questions about where I was going and which regiment I would be joining, and so on. One older man had a son who was then serving in the British Army of the Rhine (BAOR), of which I was to learn more later on, as it was the largest deployment of troops overseas at the time. So with these diversions, a catnap or two now and then, a feed of sandwiches, and an occasional cigarette (I had taken up smoking a few months before, but was not a heavy smoker at the time), the journey passed quite pleasantly.

On arrival at Oswestry station, I found there were already a number of young men waiting for the promised transport. It was easy to fall into conversation with them, and we were soon on first name terms, which seemed quite natural, since we were all destined to share the same fate! Soon the truck showed up, and a bored-looking fellow with two stripes on his sleeve told us to climb aboard. He didn't seem very friendly, but I daresay he had rounded up many such groups as ours, and was no doubt fed up with the monotony of it.

The truck journey was not long, and we were soon at the

camp gates. What greeted us there was the most dismal and depressing aspect that I had encountered up until that time. Not a tree nor a blade of grass to be seen, just rows of dilapidated and forlorn-looking huts that gave every impression of having provided temporary accommodation for soldiers en-route to the Boer War, if not, indeed, for those bound for the Crimea. On further examination though, despite their present sorry state, they showed signs of intelligent planning in their design. They were constructed in a clever arrangement known as "spiders". Each spider consisted of two 12-man huts, side by side, and joined at the center by another structure which comprised the ablutions block, with showers, toilets, wash basins etc. for use by the occupants of both huts. This proved very handy in the cool autumn weather, as it meant that there was no need to venture outside into the early morning chill for a quick scrub and shave. As far as shaving was concerned, I was fortunate in that I had a fair complexion, and a light beard growth, so that for most of my Army career I was able to get away with shaving every second day.

Anyway, the truck stopped outside one of the spiders, we disembarked, and were handed over to a sergeant who was to be our chief contact with authority for the next two weeks. He checked off our names against the list on his clipboard, then took us into the hut where we were each allocated a "bed space". Each space had a steel bed with a bare mattress, and a locker with a couple of drawers and shelves, and that was it. The next move was to be herded over to the Quarter-Master's Store, where we were issued with all we would need until the next morning, when we would get the rest of our equipment. So we now received a pillow, a couple of blankets, a set of aluminium mess tins and a huge china mug, and a set of camper-style cutlery - knife fork and spoon - which were held together by a clip when not in use. Returning to the hut, we made up our beds as well as we could, and then, the day by now being well advanced, we were directed to the mess hall for our first experience of Army food. We shuffled along the line as the disinterested-looking kitchen staff ladled the victuals into our mess tins. There was bread and butter available and well-stewed tea from a massive urn. Hunger being the best sauce, as the saying goes, and young appetites being characteristically keen, we made short work of the meal. The food, though plain, was plentiful and satisfying. It was claimed that Army rations, though frequently unappetizing were scientifically designed to provide a balanced diet adequate to sustain health and wellbeing, and this may well have been so, for in my experience, illnesses that could be blamed on dietary deficiencies were extremely rare.

The facilities for washing up the dishes, however, left much to be desired. The only provision for that was a trough of hot water to slosh the utensils about in. After a short while the water was covered by a layer of greasy scum, and as it cooled it became less and less effective, so as to become virtually useless. This was a curious departure from the Army's normal obsession with cleanliness, and I can only imagine that the intention was to expose us to a certain amount of bacteria so as to strengthen our immune systems!

After the meal we returned to our quarters, and were left to our own devices for the rest of the day, having been advised to turn in early, as on the morrow the business of soldiering would begin in earnest. For the first few nights I found it difficult to get to sleep. No doubt this was largely due to the unfamiliar surroundings- for the last few years, since my brother had left home, I had had a bedroom to myself, and now I was sharing accommodation with eleven others, some of whom were as restless as I was. Another factor was, I think, that our house in Cornwall was on the cliffs overlooking the ocean, and I was used to being lulled to sleep by the sound of waves crashing against the shore. I found the deathly silence somewhat eerie and unnerving until I got used to it.

The morning after our arrival we were awakened at daybreak by an unholy racket, as an N .C.O. clattered into the hut, banging on the beds with his swagger stick, and roaring "Wakey, wakey, rise and shine!", and various other instructions, some of them quite obscene, in a voice that ought to have roused the whole camp, if not half the villages in the surrounding countryside. This was a dawn ritual that was to become a regular feature of our new life, and signaled the start of another day of feverish activity, seemingly intended to keep us in a state of continual confusion and bewilderment.

This first morning, having hurriedly completed our ablutions and swallowed a breakfast of porridge, toast, and a mug of that strong, sweet brew so beloved of the British soldier everywhere, we spent the better part of the morning traipsing between the Q-store and the barrack-room, collecting and trying to come to terms with that huge array of largely unfamiliar items that comprise a soldier's "kit".

There were two sets of battledress-jackets and trousers-known in Army parlance as "Best B.D." and "Second Best B.D". The Best B.D. was to be kept in perfect condition, and was reserved for special parades, while the Second Best was for less formal occasions. The two pairs of boots we received were similarly treated. There was also a denim suit, to be used for the more strenuous of our activities-i.e. most of the time. There was a very heavy and well-named greatcoat, decorated in the front by a double row of brass buttons, and three smaller ones at the back, on the sort of half belt that had no practical purpose. These coats could absorb a phenomenal amount of rain, as we were to find out before long. It was said of them that it took three days for them to get soaked through, and three weeks to dry out. We were given a navy blue beret and brass cap badge, a few pairs of heavy woollen socks, three flannel shirts, three singlets and three pairs of underpants (quaintly known as "Drawers Cellular"). There was also a waterproof groundsheet, which doubled as a poncho. It was essentially a rectangular sheet with a hole in the center through which to poke one's head. The sides were then closed by means of snap fasteners to make a cape. This was very good for keeping the shoulders, back and buttocks dry, but unfortunately the water had a tendency to run down the backs of the legs, soaking the trousers and running inside the gaiters into the boots, so that after a while you would be squelching along with sopping wet feet. They made good groundsheets, though. On the second night there happened to be some heavy rain which leaked through the dilapidated roof in an annoying drip right onto my bed. So, thinking it was a good idea, I spread my groundsheet over the blanket and settled down for an exhausted sleep. As it turned out, this was a grave mistake, for the condensation thus caused made my blanket wetter than it would have been had I left well enough alone.

That was about it for clothing, and then there was the webbing equipment. This consisted of belt, gaiters (with straps and the inevitable brass buckles), big pack, small pack, water bottle holder, bayonet holder, (called, quite oddly, a "frog"), and a set of straps to hold it all together, with still more brass ends and buckles. Then there was a little white cotton folding sort of pouch, which I understand is called an etui in educated circles, but to us was known as a housewife, or more properly, a "hussif". This handy little item contained needles, thread, a hank of wool for darning socks, and a few spare buttons- everything in fact necessary for making running repairs. The final item for the time being was a large canvas kit bag, which, I was later to find, would hold an enormous amount of gear if properly packed.

When we got all this stuff back to the barrack room, we did the best we could to stack it into our lockers as neatly as possible, no easy task I might add. What wouldn't fit into the locker was folded up neatly and laid out on the bed until such time as we received more education as to its correct disposition. Over the following few days all this was made clear to us, as was the proper methods of cleaning and caring for our clothing and equipment. When we were thus fully equipped, we were each given some brown paper and string with which to pack all our civilian apparel, which would be sent to our homes at the Army's expense. We now belonged completely and wholly to the Army, upon which we depended totally.

Each hut was provided with an electric iron, which we found to be invaluable, not only for pressing shirts and B.D.'s, but also for the process of" bulling" boots. This was an arduous task, which took literally hours. The boots were made of chrome leather, which had a very bumpy and uneven surface. This had to be levelled off before the requisite sheen could be achieved. The way to do this was to apply a liberal layer of Cherry Blossom boot polish to the surface of the boot, and then burn it into the leather with the hot iron. When the surface had been nicely evened off, the actual "bulling" could begin. This tedious and time consuming business was performed by spitting on the boot, and then applying a good dollop of polish with a cloth, and gently rubbing it in, in the proverbial "small circles". Hence the expression "spit and polish". Many repetitive hours of "bulling" resulted in a mirror-like finish in which the Sergeant could literally see his face, and thus leave you alone for a while. Fortunately only the Best Boots had to receive this treatment- the Second Best ones just had to be cleaned with brushes and polish in the normal way.

Another miserable job was treating the webbing gear. This was done by using a queer substance called "Blanco". This came in a dry block of a greenish colour, which when moistened with a wet brush to form a paste could then be applied to the webbing in as even layer as possible, and then allowed to dry. The worst problem with Blanco was that it got all over the brasswork, especially the buckles, and had to be carefully removed before applying the Brasso.

After a good couple of applications of Blanco the webbing gear didn't require much attention for quite a while, but not so with the brass, which needed polishing every day. The worst parts of the brassware were the greatcoat buttons and of course the cap badge. For the buttons we were supplied with a "button stick". This was a thin brass plate with a narrow slot for most of its length, which slid under the button and so prevented the polish from staining the fabric. The badge could of course be removed for cleaning. I have to say that Blanco was an extremely durable substance-once it was thoroughly ingrained into the webbing equipment, it was very difficult to shift. Later on, when I was stationed with a regular regiment, I knew one bloke who had spent a month in the detention camp in Colchester. Instead of the normal green Blanco, in Colchester they used a different coloured stuff, a sort of sandy shade. When he had served his sentence and returned to the regiment, it took him several hard scrubbing sessions and a few applications of the green Blanco before his webbing gear returned to the proper colour.

The standard issue greatcoat buttons were decorated with the Royal crest, but there were special Artillery buttons which had on them instead a gun surmounted by a crown. These were quite predictably called gun buttons, and since they were not standard issue, had to be purchased. We were told that while we could not be compelled to spend our own money in this way, it was felt that as a matter of regimental pride we would naturally wish to do so. Furthermore it was made perfectly clear to us that things would go ill for anyone on the next parade whose greatcoat was not adorned with a set of highly burnished gun buttons.

On the matter of pride in the regiment, great efforts were made to instill this into us. Our sergeant, early on in the piece, was at pains to insist that we were never to think of ourselves as mere privates-we were Gunners, an infinitely superior life-form, difficult as that might be to believe when looking at the sorry shower with which he, for his sins, had been so cruelly lumbered. He vowed however, that notwithstanding the near im-possibility of the task, he was determined to do his sacred duty, and somehow make out of us not only soldiers, but gunners! On the same theme, he reminded us that there were no corporals in the Artillery. Our N.C.O.'s were Bombardiers, and must always be addressed as such.

Our cap badge, he insisted, said it all. The R.A. badge features a crown and a gun and scrolls bearing the Latin legend "UBIQUE QUO FAS ET GLORIA DUCUNT ", which translates into English thus- "EVERYWHERE WHERE RIGHT AND GLORY LEAD". We were reminded that that the Artillery had served with distinction in every major conflict involving the

British Army, from the Battle of Crecy in 1346 to the present war in Korea. While the infantry peasants might make derogatory remarks about seven mile snipers, and marching on wheels and so on, our proud claim was that the Artillery lends dignity to what would otherwise be a common brawl.

Over the next few weeks we were treated to more such entertaining lectures on the subject of regimental history (some would say brainwashing), very welcome interludes in the hurly-burly of frenetic physical activity that occupied most of our time. We learned for example that the Artillery is unique in that it is a Regimental Corps, the full title of which is the Royal Regiment of Artillery. There are several sections of this body, such as Light, Medium, Heavy, Anti-aircraft, Coastal, and Locating, according to the equipment they use, and its purpose. The individual units comprising the whole are called regiments, which correspond to the battalions of the infantry. Each regiment is divided into batteries and troops, rather than companies and platoons as in the infantry. There is one special group known as the Royal Horse Artillery. All I know about them is that their cap badge was of the same design as ours, but much larger, and that the gun wheel turns, making the badge harder to polish when the Brasso gets in behind the wheel.

As I say, all this information was drummed into us as a means of instilling in us a sense of pride in, and loyalty to the proud legacy to which we were heirs. The British Army obviously set great store by the philosophy underlying this strategy. A long time ago the practice of numbering regiments had been abandoned in favour of giving them names which linked them to specific geographical regions, especially to particular counties. Thus we have the Somerset Light Infantry, the Northumberland Fusiliers, the Hampshire Regiment, the King's Own Scottish

Borderers, the Lancashire Fusiliers, and many, many others with similar designations. Sadly, in recent years, in the interests of rationilisation, some of these regiments have been amalgamated and so to some extent have lost their original proud identities. However, as far as I was concerned such sentimental reflections lay far in the future. For the moment sheer survival was a far greater problem. The primary object of our N .C.O.'s seemed to be to strip us completely of any sense of identity or self-esteem. We were subjected to a constant stream of verbal abuse, some of it quite colourful and imaginative. Doubts were cast upon our ancestry, and our intelligence or rather our lack of it. No effort was spared to make us feel that we were absolutely and utterly useless and an embarrassment to the human race.

One effect of this, whether intentional or not, was to create a bond between us, so that we felt that we, the oppressed were united against the common enemy, the authorities. Thus we sympathized when one of us was singled out for abuse, since an attack on one was seen as an attack on all. The days passed in a blur of bewilderment and confusion as our sergeant and bombardiers took turns to ensure that moments of leisure were kept to a minimum.

No doubt because they were required by law to do so, the authorities were at great pains to assure us that if we had any complaints relating to the conditions in which we were obliged to live, or concerning the treatment we received, then we were fully entitled to contact our M.P.'s (Members of Parliament that is, not Military Police!), for help in resolving the issues. At the same time it was none too subtly hinted that anyone incautious enough to avail himself of this privilege would be afforded ample opportunity and cause to rue the folly of his action. Needless to say, it was tacitly accepted that, discretion being infinitely the better part of valor, the wisest course would be to roll with the punches, and suffer in silence!

Not all was doom and gloom though, there were lighter moments too. Like the time quite early in the proceedings when we were marched in batches to the camp barber's shop for our first acquaintance with Army hair styling. This was very simple- it consisted of removing virtually all the hair, leaving only a very short stubble, like a day's growth, all over the head. Some of the city blokes were close to tears, watching in horror as their luxuriant locks fell in heaps at the barber's feet. Many of them had to make adjustments to the headbands of their berets to get them to fit snugly. There was much general hilarity at everybody's changed appearance, with raucous speculation as to whose new look was the most ridiculous. One beneficial effect of it all was that the shared humiliation brought us all closer together, and we became a more cohesive group as a result.

The comprehensive nature of conscription meant that recruits came from all levels of society, and from all parts of the country. It took me a fair while to learn to distinguish between the huge variety of accents, dialects and idiom into which the English language is divided. I had long been familiar, from films and radio, with the better known and recognisable accents, such as Cockney and Scottish, but there so many more that I had never heard before. Probably this situation was less common in the infantry regiments, which, being territorially based, drew most of their personnel from their own district, while the Artillery, like the Service Corps, Ordnance Corps and other similar organisations, cast a wider net.

After a while though, I became more accustomed to the various tones, and could distinguish quite readily between Geordie and Scouse, Brummie and Taffy, or Yorkie and other northern accents. We had in our number one bloke from the Scottish Islands — either the Hebrides or the Orkneys, I can't remember which, and he had a wonderfully musical lilt in his speech, very easy on the ears. It was in stark contrast to the rather harsher tones of Glasgow or Edinburgh.

There were a couple of blokes from the Isle of Man, one of whom was a kipper- smoker from Peel. He was an outgoing character, who often held forth at some length, and considerable passion, on the superior quality of Manx kippers compared to those from anywhere else. Manx kippers, he said, were properly smoked, using traditional and time-honoured methods, while other producers elsewhere resorted to the deceitful trick of using dye to make their kippers look more attractive, a despicable practice that would never be countenanced on the Isle of Man! This same chap was a born entertainer, and a very good singer. He enlivened many an evening for us with his repertoire of popular songs. There was another interesting bloke, who was a jockey in civilian life; he had a few fascinating yarns to tell about life in the racing game. His military career, however, was very short, for he was discharged on medical grounds even before the fortnight was up. I never found out what the problem was, and how he managed to pass the stringent pre-enlistment medical was something of a mystery.

The training regime at Oswestry was basic, and designed to familiarise recruits with the fundamentals of Army life - the use and care of the equipment, for example, and with parade ground drill, or square-bashing to use the Army vernacular. There was no technical training, just the sort of stuff all soldiers learned, whatever branch they might later be assigned to. Much of the two weeks there passed in a kind of blur, filled as they were with frantic activity leaving little time for contemplation. As a break from square-bashing there would be periods of physical training in the gym, chinning the bar, press-ups, leaping over the vaulting horse, shinning up the ropes which hung down from the ceiling and all the rest of the usual exercises, most of which were familiar from schooldays. Our instructor, a bombardier, was a very impressive figure, built like a middleweight boxer, and very muscular. He was able to climb the rope with the agility of a monkey, using only one hand and his feet to shin up to the top. He could also do press-ups with one hand, and seemed to possess unlimited stamina. Fortunately he was aware of our limitations, and did not expect us follow his example!

At last, in the manner of all things, good or bad, our time at Oswestry came to an end. By now despite the state of humiliation, bewilderment, intimidation, and occasional abject terror in which we had existed for the past fourteen days, most of us had absorbed a modicum of understanding of what the military was all about, and were deemed to be ready for the next phase.

This would consist of eight weeks of intense training, which would not only perfect the lessons we had already learned, but also include the more involved manoeuvres, such as rifle drill as well as the introduction of the technical aspects of the trade which we were to follow.

On our last day the group we were assembled on parade, and for the first time learned our new destinations. I have no idea on what basis it was decided who should go where, but I found that I was to proceed to an Anti-Aircraft training regiment at Tonfanau, a small settlement on the Welsh coast, near Towyn in the county of Merioneth, and that I would be trained as a radar operator.

3

THE TRAINED SOLDIER

The camp at Tonfanau presented the same sort of bleak, desolate aspect that seems to be the prevailing characteristic of all Army establishments — row after row of wooden huts in barren sur-roundings, and very little else. This camp, however was of more recent vintage than Oswestry. The huts were free-standing, each designed to accommodate twelve men — a number that seemed to be a favourite with the Army. The ablution block was a separate building, which meant early morning exposure to the elements. At least the buildings were water-proof, which was an improvement. The experiences that I had endured at Oswestry had been something of a culture shock to me, after the freedom and comfort of civilian life in a relaxed atmosphere of a small country town. To be suddenly pitch-forked into a situation where everything was done "at the double", in bursts of frenetic activity, had been bad enough, but in comparison to what was to come at Tonfanau, the two weeks at Oswestry had been like a fortnight at one of Billy Butlin's holiday camps. Here they were really serious about it!

For all activities except technical subjects and gym training, we were given into the care of a triumvirate of N.C.O.'s, a sergeant, a bombardier, and a lance - bombardier, all of whom we came to know very well in the ensuing weeks as the "Unholy Trinity". The first was Sgt. Murray, a dour, abrasive Scotsman, rather small of stature, but tough as an old boot. The rows of medal ribbons on his chest suggested that he had had a lively time of it during the war. I suppose he would have been in his early thirties, but to us young sprogs he looked much older. (At the time, anyone over thirty was generally known as "Pop"). Sgt. Murray was a strict, uncompromising, even harsh disciplinarian, but scrupulously fair, so that every one of us incurred his wrath sooner or later. I had my share at least twice.

The first occasion was on parade one morning. We were drawn up in three ranks as usual, for the preliminary inspection before the drill began, when the state of the brass buckles on my belt failed to meet his standards. So I was marched out in front of the squad, and ordered to take off my belt and drop it on the ground. Then I was instructed to mark time on it, while he returned to the others and carried on with the drill. After a while, thinking to minimize the damage, I moved ever so slightly forward, so that I was no longer stamping on the belt. But this manoeuvre turned out to be a miscalculation, for the sergeant immediately spotted what I was up to , and ordered me to resume the correct position, adding that for my insolence the punishment would be extended for another five minutes. The state of the belt after such brutal treatment as being stomped on by heavy hob-nailed boots for such a long period, can well be imagined. It took me more than two hours of hard work to restore it to its normal condition.

The brasswork was of course badly scratched, and required many applications of Brasso and much elbow grease to achieve an acceptable shine, and the webbing needed a couple of coats of Blanco. On another occasion, obviously having decided that it was my turn again, the sergeant once more selected me for special treatment. Every morning we had to make our beds and arrange our kit on it in a particular, strictly enforced pattern.

The mattress cover had to be stretched tightly over the mattress, so tightly that a half-crown dropped on it would bounce. The "hospital corners" had to be just so, the bedding to be neatly folded and placed at the head of the bed, and the kit laid out in the prescribed fashion. For example, socks had to be rolled in such a way as to measure exactly four inches by four inches. Even the hussif had to be neat, opened out to show that every needle was in its proper place. The Best Boots were on display, highly polished all Over, even the soles! — And mess kit impeccably scoured. The attention to detail was nothing short of phenomenal.

Well, on this particular day something, I had no idea what, must have caught the sergeant's eye, and so displeased him that he poked his swagger stick under the mattress, and tipped the whole lot onto the floor. What a performance it was to sort that out into some semblance of order, especially in view of the limited time allowed for the exercise. I didn't feel so badly about it this time though, because this little trick was one of Sgt. Murray's favourites, and most of us copped it sooner or later. So there wasn't anything personal about it! The belt-stomping episode on the other hand had been a one-off exhibition of pure spite! Sgt. Murray had a favourite expression which he used whenever he suspected that someone was being less than truthful with him. He would roar: "Dinna tell me falsehoods — I'm no' a man tae be told bloody falsehoods tae!" Although most of the time Sgt. Murray came through as something of a martinet, looking back I think that he was basically a very decent person. He had a difficult job to do, and he did it pretty well. It was just that because of our position relative to his, we rarely saw the human side of his personality. He did have a lighter side though, which showed through every now and then.

On parade he would occasionally come out with one of the old, time-honoured quips, most of which he must have heard for the first time when he himself was a raw recruit many years before. Little gems like:

"Did you use a mirror to shave with this morning?"

"Yes, Sergeant."

"Well, in future use a bloody razor!", or:

"Did you use a razor this morning?"

"Yes, Sergeant."

"Well, put a blade in it next time!", or:

"Well, stand a bit closer to it tomorrow!"

One day we were in the lecture hall, undergoing a bit of brain washing and keeping out of the weather, when the bombardier burst in, shaking water off his poncho and announced "It's raining cats and dogs out there!" to which Sgt. Murray's straight faced reply was 'Och well, I hope ye didn'ae step in a poodle!"

In common with many of his contemporaries, Sgt. Murray had a disdain for junior officers, especially those who were National Servicemen. They were considered to be dilettantes, little more than a waste of space, (an opinion with which most of us heartily agreed, I hasten to add), and no chance of embarrassing them was missed. It was customary for mail to be distributed to the rabble at the end of morning parade, while we were still in three ranks. The Sergeant would have a sheaf of letters in his hand, and would deal them out as you would a pack of cards. He would call the recipient's name, and hearing the response, would flick the envelope in the direction of the voice. This he would do with astounding accuracy, and it was seldom indeed that anyone had to break ranks to retrieve the letter. If there happened to be one of the sprog officers in attendance, he would start off as usual, "Gnr, Smith, Gnr. Jones, Gnr. Williams", and so on, and then would come "Gonorrhoea" — no response — "GONORRHOEA", to the delight of the mob and the acute discomfiture of the officer, unaccustomed as he was to such uncouth humour. Despite his often abrasive manner, Sgt. Murray commanded a great deal of respect and by the time our eight weeks at Tonfanau were up, he was held in high regard, if not actual affection. The man had character. Bombardier Frampton was of a different ilk. He was something of an enigma, being of uncertain temper, and less predictable than Sgt. Murray. At least with Murray you knew where you stood. The bombardier soon acquired the nickname "The Frampire" from his rather convoluted warning that he intended to draw blood from us by drilling us so hard on the parade ground that our feet would bleed. He too was a "Regular", but by no means as dedicated to the cause as the Sergeant. He had a curious way of wearing his beret, quite in contravention of the rules of proper dress. The regulation way was to arrange the headgear so that the badge sat directly above the left eye, the edge of the beret to be an inch above the eyebrows and parallel to the ground, and the right side pulled down over the right ear. With the Frampire, however, the badge sat over the centre of his forehead, and the sides pulled down equally over each ear. In fact, this arrangement presented a more symmetrical effect than the official way, but was nevertheless an infringement of the dress code. It was a matter of conjecture how he managed to get away with it, but naturally none of us was game to raise the issue. The third member of the triumvirate was Lance-Bombardier Taylor. He was an innocuous sort of bloke, a National Serviceman like us, and did not pose too much of a threat, or cause us too much bother.

There was a Second-Lieutenant nominally in charge of the squad, but he was never much in evidence, preferring to leave control of the rabble in the hands of the N.C.O's. He too was an NS man, a product of Mons officer school rather than the more prestigious Sandhurst, and was considered to be an amateur, unworthy of much respect. Once or twice he was required to give us a lecture on regimental history, but since he knew rather less about the subject than we did, these sessions, though providing a welcome break from square-bashing, were largely a waste of time.

Our technical training as radar operators began at this time as well, and for this we had a specially qualified instructor, a sergeant. He was a very pleasant fellow, unusually so for a Regular! Apart from trying to get us to understand the fundamentals of operating this mysterious machine, he would often regale us with tales of his experiences in Hong Kong, where he had served for several years. From the fond way he spoke of the place, he was obviously in love with Hong Kong, and in fact told us that as soon as his time in the Army was finished, a couple of years hence, he intended to go there to live.

The radar set was housed in a large trailer, and the interior was big enough to accommodate five people, so we could be trained four at a time. It would become quite warm and cosy in there, and without the diversion of the sergeant's yarns, it is likely we would have dozed off eventually though we managed to absorb enough of the complexities of these marvellous machines to make at least some sense of it all.

As in all military establishments, rumours abounded at Tonfanau. One of these told of a dramatic incident a few months previously, which resulted in the loss of an aeroplane. It seemed that the radar operator had mistakenly latched onto the plane itself, instead of the target sleeve it was towing. With commendable accuracy the gun crew had loosed off a salvo which had caused the plane, still towing the target, to plummet into the chilly waters of Cardigan Bay. Fortunately the pilot had managed to bail out in time, and was picked up, spluttering, shivering and cursing, by a rescue launch. We were warned against ever repeating the error, for the R.A.F. people were still very unhappy about the mishap.

Another rumour asserted that a member of a recent intake, being unable to tolerate the severe stress imposed by the training schedule had taken his own life, poor chap. We were gravely advised not to follow this course of action either, since both it and the aeroplane incident involved the destruction of Government property, very serious offences indeed, and ones which would incur severe penalties. There was of course no way for us either to verify or to disprove these stories, but the earnestness with which they were related suggested that an open display of scepticism would be considered inappropriate.

Over time I realised that Army life is riddled with rumours and scare- mongering, designed largely to keep the inexperienced and unwary in a constant state of uncertainty. After a while I developed a philosophy based on an old Irish saying, "Hope for the best and provide against the worst." In this way, any surprises were likely to be pleasant ones.

The most diverting experience of this period was our introduction to firearms. Initially this took the form of sessions in the indoor firing range, using .22 rifles at fairly close range, and aiming at targets backed by sandbags. This obviously was to get us accustomed to the noise and feel of the rifle. We would each fire five rounds, with varying levels of success. Having satisfied the instructor that we were unlikely to shoot either ourselves or any innocent bystanders, we were soon promoted to the outdoor range. There we would become acquainted with the mainstay of the British Army, the famous Lee Enfield .303, with which we were to develop an intimate relationship in the following weeks, both on the firing range and the parade ground.

The .303 is a bolt-action weapon with a ten round magazine. The bullets are normally held in clips of five rounds, and the reloading is done by inserting the clip into the breech of the rifle, and pushing the bullets down into the magazine with the thumb. The clip can then be recharged or discarded.

On the range the firing line was 100 yards from the targets, which were set up on steel frames and were raised and lowered manually by the "butt party", who sheltered in a kind of bunker below the targets. As the target was hit, the bloke in the butts would indicate the position of the bullet hole with a pointed arrow on a stick, so that the rifleman could adjust his aim. After five rounds the target was lowered and the bullet holes covered with sticky tape, then raised again for the next shooter. When then target was so badly battered, that it was only held together by the tape, it was replaced by a new one.

It could be a trifle nerve-racking in the butts, because occasionally a badly aimed bullet would ricochet off the steel framework, and fly off in any direction. There were, however, no casualties as far as I ever heard.

It had long been part of Army lore that it is a mistake to show exceptional competence with a rifle. If you do, the likelihood is that you will end up as a sniper, a lonely and dangerous occupation with a depressingly short life expectancy. As far as our group was concerned, our very average performance, despite our best efforts, made it seem unlikely that such a fate would befall any of us, though most of us did enjoy our forays onto the range.

As well as the diversion of these shooting parties, there was of course the less entertaining business of rifle drill on the parade ground. It must have taken the mind of a twisted genius to devise the intricate and complicated sequence of manoeuvres involved in this exercise in futility. There are commands such as "Order arms", "Slope arms", "Trail arms", "Ground arms", "Present as a salute), and the ominous "For inspection, port arms", all of which, unintelligible to the uninitiated, must be followed by the appropriate action, promptly and precisely. For inspection the breech had to be opened and the bolt operated five times to ensure any overlooked bullets were expelled, and as the inspecting officer reached you, you had to bring the rifle around to face forward. At the same time you had to stick your thumb into the breech. This enabled the officer to peer down the barrel to make sure of its cleanliness, as the reflection of light from your thumbnail illuminated the bore and showed up any specks of dirt or other signs of neglect.

Rifles had to be cleaned regularly, by use of the "pull-through." The pull-through was a length of heavy cord with a weight at one end and a loop at the other. Into the loop was threaded a piece of linen cloth called a "four by two", from its dimensions in inches. A drop of oil was applied to this, then the weight placed in the breech and shaken down so that it pulled the cord through the barrel, until the four by two was in the breech. Then the weight was grasped and pulled with a smooth, even movement without a pause — otherwise a mark would be left in the bore. So that they were always available, the pull-through, four by two and oil bottle were carried in a cavity in the rifle butt, which had a brass butt plate with a hinged trap door.

In time, of course, constant repetition and the "none too gentle encouragement" of the sergeant, ensured that all the drills became second nature, and commands were responded to with alacrity and an acceptable degree of precision. At last, when we were brought to attention, the crash of our boots on the parade ground began to sound more like a rifle shot and less like a burst of machine gun fire.

So the days passed quite rapidly, what with drill, technical training, the occasional morale-boosting lecture, route marches, kit inspections, endless cleaning, polishing; in short all the paraphernalia familiar to anyone who has ever seen a film about army life. Except that it is a bit different living through it, instead of witnessing other people's misery!

Physical Training (P. T.) sessions were generally held in the morning immediately after breakfast. I'm sure that as we marched to the gym, clad in shorts, singlet, gym shoes and greatcoats in the chilly autumn dawn, we must have resembled nothing as much as Napoleon' s demoralised Grande Armee on its retreat from Moscow. Most of us were familiar with exercises from our P.T. lessons at school, and had little trouble in performing adequately. But there was one bloke who had great difficulty in chinning the bar. He was somewhat overweight, an unusual condition among young people in that era, since we had been raised in the dark days of food shortages and rationing, especially of sugar and luxuries like sweets and ice cream. It was pitiful to see this chap struggle manfully to get his feet off the ground, grunting and sweating. Press-ups were equally painful for him.

One event in particular stands out in my memories of Tonfanau, and that is the time I fell afoul of the Regimental Sergeant-Major. Now I should explain that the R.S.M. occupies a special place in the hierarchy of the regiment. The position is unique, more important in many ways than the C.O. himself. He is often referred to as the kingpin of the regiment, and is held in fear and awe by all ranks below that of captain, perhaps particularly by the junior officers!

Well, one evening I was making my back from the NAAFI, along the edge of the barrack square (it is strictly forbidden to set foot on the sacred surface of the square itself except when on parade), when I saw in the dim light a tall imposing figure approaching from the opposite direction. I could just make out that he was wearing a peaked cap, rather than the dark blue beret worn by the so-called "other ranks." Thinking therefore that this must be an officer, I threw up a smart salute as we passed. I was halted in my tracks by a stentorian roar that must have set every watchdog for miles around barking furiously, not to mention startling the local populace out of ten years' growth. I realised with horror that this was none other than the dreaded R.S.M. himself. He proceeded to treat me to a diatribe using every term of abuse to which he could lay his tongue (his vocabulary was phenomenal), including in detail some facts about my ancestry of which had hitherto been blissfully unaware.

Having run out of breath, and spent his wrath, he stormed off, leaving me still quaking, but mercifully without inflicting any additional punishment. In my confusion I had forgotten that in spite of his elevated Status, an R.S.M. is not to be saluted — the salute is a courtesy accorded only to commissioned officers.

In any case I had not noticed in the fading light the brightly polished brass cap badge, which is the main distinguishing feature between the headgear of an R. S. M. and that of an officer, whose badge is of a dull bronze colour. My roommates had a good laugh at my expense when I told them of my humiliation.

One day, by way of a change of routine, we were invited to form a Rugby team to play a "friendly" against the regiment's representative fifteen, which we knew to have a formidable record in inter-unit competition. Nothing daunted, we scraped together enough of our people with some knowledge of the game to make up a team, and on a wet and windy Saturday afternoon took the field against our opponents, who by all appearances outweighed us by an average of at least two stone apiece. They also had the advantage of having played together as a team for a season or two. The result was predictable — we received a severe thrashing, by exactly how much we never knew because nobody bothered to keep score, but it was a lot. I did have one moment of glory though. I was playing at full-back, and suddenly one of their forwards broke free of the pack, and stormed towards me, confident of scoring yet another try. In sheer desperation and suicidal determination, I wrapped my skinny arms around his massive legs, and brought him crashing to the ground, thus temporarily stemming the tide. The mismatch finally ended, and battered and battle- weary, we returned to barracks, there to spend the next couple of hours repairing the damage to our gear. In the absence of proper sports gear we had been obliged to wear our gym shorts, singlets and second best boots, which had suffered badly in the muddy conditions. The boots in particular needed some work, since they were not only wet and dirty, but also badly scuffed. But despite everything it was generally agreed that it had been good fun, and well worth-while.

It was customary on the last weekend to grant passes to the recruits to visit the neighboring town for a few hours, as some kind of compensation perhaps for the agony of degradation we had undergone. Actually, it is amazing how quickly one adjusts to a radical change in life-style — by now I had become so accustomed to the frantic pace of activity that is the recruit's lot, that it seemed almost normal. I no longer resented the constant harrying and rushing about — even beginning in a perverse kind of way to get some enjoyment out of it. I was beginning to become a soldier!

There was one of our number who fancied himself as a bit of a Casanova, and in anticipation of a conquest or two in Towyn, he had for the last month refrained from drinking tea, on the grounds that the tea served at mealtimes was heavily laced with bromide, which was widely supposed to suppress the libido, and he did not wish to put himself at a disadvantage. However, as so often happens in the Army, his scheme came to nought. The day before the long-awaited leave, our would-be Lothario, having been found guilty of some minor offence, had his leave pass cancelled, and he was assigned instead to cookhouse fatigues for the weekend.

Traditionally cookhouse fatigues have been associated with peeling potatoes - spud-bashing in Army parlance. Spud-bashing was generally thought to be a soul- destroying business, but I never found it so. At least it was a sedentary occupation, and as it required little mental exertion, left the mind free to wander. Much more unpleasant to me was the so-called pan wash. This hateful task involved scrubbing huge, filthy, grease-encrusted roasting pans in a tub of hot water, on which there soon formed a revolting scum. This found its way under the fingernails, and took days to get rid of.

As far as the trip to Towyn is concerned, it was a big disap-pointment anyway. The shortage of disposable income, common to soldiers throughout history, was naturally an inhibiting factor. Furthermore the attitude of the local people was less than inviting. Most of them studiously avoided speaking English unless it was absolutely necessary. It appeared that anti-English sentiment was alive and well in these parts. Perhaps too they were weary of having their peace shattered periodically by the invading hordes of boisterous teenagers.

One day as a change from the usual routine, we were herded

into the lecture hall to hear an address by an officer from the Parachute Regiment. When we were all comfortably seated, there came a sound from the back of the hall — "Clump, clump, clump", and the visiting officer appeared, his right leg encased in a heavy plaster cast, and complete with walking stick, and wearing the famous "Red Beret." He explained at the outset that his disability was the result of an accident in a Rugby match, and then delivered an inspiring lecture on the benefits of joining the "Paras." Not only was there the prestige of belonging to an elite regiment, but there was also the inducement of extra pay, in the form of what was called "jump pay." In order to retain the bonus it was necessary to leap out of an aeroplane every so often, so as to maintain enthusiasm and efficiency, and presumably one's nerve. It all sounded very exciting, but unfortunately for the recruitment drive, the damage had already been done. The image of the plaster cast was a powerful and lasting one, despite the account of the football mishap, with the result that there were in the event no volunteers from our squad. Most of us were NS men, and our main objective was to emerge unscathed at the end of our two year stint.

A day or two before we were to disperse to our new regiments, having survived eight weeks of the most intense experience I had ever encountered, came the glorious occasion of the passing-out parade, When we would finally cease to be recruits, and become soldiers. I have wondered at times why this important ceremony was called "passing-out." I don't think it had anything to do with the fact that occasionally someone would literally pass out in a faint after standing at attention for what seemed like hours waiting for the appearance of the inspecting officer. While this did happen, it was not such a frequent phenomenon as to give its name to the whole ceremony. Incidentally, we had previously been advised by Sgt. Murray that the best way to avoid such an embarrassing disaster was, very gently and perforce unnoticeably, to raise the heels slightly so as to take the weight off them, putting the strain instead on the balls of the feet. It was thought that the stress on the spine was thus relieved, preventing oxygen starvation to the brain. Whatever the science of it, it seemed to work quite well.

The parade itself was quite nerve-racking — the expectations of our N .C.O.'s were high, and we had found from experience that it was bad policy to disappoint them. In the event, however, everything went without incident, and everyone concerned was well pleased with the outcome. The inspection and the drill display being completed, we were ready to march off the parade ground and return to barracks. It was a pleasant surprise to hear Sgt. Murray give the commands in a voice with more than a touch of pride "Trained soldiers, right turn. Trained soldiers, by the right, quick march!"

I should explain that as recruits we had been obliged to swing our arms to shoulder height as we marched. Now, as trained soldiers, we were allowed to swing only to waist height. A small point to be sure, but to us a great source of satisfaction.

We had earlier taken up a collection from our meagre pay, with which we had bought a small gift for each of our N.C.O.'s, and these were now presented with appropriate expressions of appreciation for their patience and forbearance over the past two months. This had been at considerable financial sacrifice on our part, for although it was the Army's proud boast that they would "make men of us", it had become painfully clear at our first pay parade that there was no intention of making rich men of us!

In an earlier century it had been the tradition that the British soldier would be willing to fight "for King and Country, and a

Shilling a day." By 1952, due to inflation in line with the cost of living, the rate had increased to four shillings a day for the new recruit. This amounted to twenty-eight shillings for a seven day week, there being no provision for penalty rates or overtime. Moreover we were on call twenty four hours a day, so the hourly rate would make a union steward shudder.

Out of the 28 shillings there was a deduction of three shillings a week for National Insurance, and a further shilling to cover "barrack room damages." This last was an absolute swindle, for if there was any damage, such as a broken window, it had to be paid for by the occupants anyway. Out of the remaining 24 bob we had to buy Brasso, Blanco, and other cleaning gear, so it is not surprising that payday was eagerly awaited each week.

At the end of six months there would be an increase to five shillings a day, and after a year yet another increase to seven. On the completion of eighteen months' service, as long as conduct had been satisfactory, the soldier qualified for a third "star", and for his last six months would receive the princely sum of ten shillings a day, three pounds ten a week! — Wealth beyond the dreams of avarice!

This was at a time when a farm labourer living in a rent free tied cottage got about six pounds for a forty-four hour week, and a tradesman's pay was in the order of eleven pounds. However, to be fair it should be noted that we received free room and board and free clothing and equipment. Medical and dental treatment were also free of charge, so altogether we weren't too badly off.

Anyway, all the harassment and abuse we had suffered during our ordeal was forgotten, or at least forgiven, in the euphoria of our new status, and the anticipation of our forthcoming postings to our new regiments. One of our number, a Yorkshireman who had played a few games for Bradford, was retained on the

Permanent Staff, in order to boost the strength of the regimental soccer team, while the rest of us were to be transferred, in an apparently haphazard manner, to various units all over the country, presumably to wherever there was a vacancy.

Together with another Cornishman, one of the few I met during my Army career, I was assigned to a regiment stationed on the Salisbury Plain. The following day we bade farewell to our comrades, with some regrets, for shared hardships had formed a few bonds, and dispersed to our various destinations. In the waiting room at Tonfanau station there was a poignant inscription on the wall:

"Roll on death, demob is far away" — not an altogether comforting or inspirational observation!

4

LARKHILL

In due course Harper and I arrived at the 52nd. Field Locating Regt. at Larkhill, on the windswept Salisbury Plain. The camp was not far from the well-known Larkhill racecourse, and in the vicinity also of Stonehenge, neither of which I was able to visit in the mercifully short time I was at the 52nd. Salisbury Plain in winter is not a particularly pleasant place, at least not for one who was raised in the more equable clime of the Cornish Riviera, and it was now nearing the end of November.

For the first couple of weeks Harper and I were billeted in a barrack room occupied by the camp cooks; apparently this was the only accommodation available for us at the time. The cooks were a very clannish and unfriendly bunch. They kept the most outlandish hours as well, being required of course to rise an hour or more ahead of the normal reveille time to prepare breakfast for the "real" soldiers. Accordingly their "lights out" was also earlier than we would have liked. We were therefore very pleased when a couple of beds became vacant in the Gunners' quarters. The cooks belonged to the Army Catering Corps, which is one of the few Corps not dignified by the prefix "Royal", and which is generally scorned by other soldiers, being classed as worthy of little more respect than the hated Military Police. Perhaps that is why they tended to adopt a rather defensive and resentful attitude.

Unlike the AA units, the 52nd. 's role was to detect enemy gun and perhaps tank movements and whatnot — I never found out precisely how they went about it, because it was evidently not the practice to conduct field manoeuvres, known in the British Army as "schemes", and by the Americans as "problems", during the winter months.

We did have one field exercise in which we were to masquerade as infantrymen, and attempt to capture an enemy stronghold. For this operation, I was nominated as Bren gunner, and was obliged to lug this cumbersome brute of a thing over rough ground at full tilt. I don't remember whether or not we succeeded in our mission, but I would suspect probably not. I suppose the idea of such a fruitless endeavour was to remind us that we were primarily soldiers, and that there was a possibility, however remote, that we might one day be called upon to display some proficiency in infantry tactics.

On the same occasion, the weather being unusually mild for the time of year, we received instruction in the correct way to carry a wounded comrade to safety, using what was known as the "fireman's lift." My partner for this exercise was a tall, raw-boned fellow, and when he grabbed me and hoisted me over his back, his bony shoulder ground into my groin, causing me such acute, eye-watering agony as he lumbered over the uneven terrain that I was left wondering how any genuinely' wounded soldier would ever survive this kind of rough handling. He never said, when it was my turn to rescue him, whether it had been a similarly painful experience for my mate Harper, a friendly and personable sort of bloke. He was a devout Christian, and one Sunday he persuaded me to accompany him to the service at the local Anglican Church. This particular church happened to adhere to the High Church ritual.

Having been raised as a Wesleyan Methodist, and therefore used to a simple form of service, often conducted by a lay preacher in the absence elsewhere of the minister, I found the priest's rich vestments and the use of incense, as well as the elaborate ritual, rather oppressive. There were not many practicing churchgoers of any denomination in our group- they were mostly a godless mob. At least that's what it looked like, but it was hard to tell for sure. Religion and politics were taboo subjects in the Army, as it was felt that both were too prone to exciting strong feelings of antagonism, so much so that many wars had been fought in their name. So these topics were rarely discussed, perhaps less because they were forbidden than because of lack of interest! Girls, football and next week's payday were matters of far greater importance!

The Army set great store in knowing everyone's religion — the main reason was probably so that battlefield casualties could be buried with the appropriate rites. With this in view, the identity discs, known as dog-tags, which we wore on a cord around our necks, were stamped with number, rank and religion. Anyone who disavowed any religious beliefs whatsoever was automatically classed as Church of England. Obviously the Army's philosophy was, as expressed by one grizzled old veteran, "there are no atheists in the trenches!"

Once in a while there would be a clean-up parade, when a fatigue party would be detailed to scour the camp and pick up any stray rubbish lying about. On one of these occasions I noticed that the pile of coal had been whitewashed. My first thought at the sight was the old Army formula for dealing with any unsightly object — "If you can't move it, paint it, and if it moves by itself, salute it." Later I discovered that this odd practice was not merely for aesthetic reasons, but had a more pragmatic purpose.

The coal was for the occupants of the married quarters for heating and cooking purposes. The idea of the whitewash was to discourage pilfering — if any coal was removed, it would leave a gaping black hole. A quick examination of the coal cellars in the married quarters would readily expose the culprit. After each coal issue the remaining pile was whitewashed again, and so it went on.

The most irksome and soul-destroying exercise in the Army was guard duty. During the daytime hours sentry duty on the main gate was the responsibility of the Regimental Police, people specially trained for the purpose. These fellows were Artillery personnel, distinct from the Royal Military Police, and did not attract the same degree of odium as the latter. The R.P.'s were decent enough blokes, and didn't go about looking for trouble. But they went off duty at six p.m., and were replaced by ordinary squaddies until six o'clock the next morning.

The guard detail consisted of seven Gunners and the guard commander, usually a junior N.C.O. In overall charge was the Orderly Officer, but he took no further part in proceedings after the Guard Mounting Parade, which was held at 5.30 p.m., or to conform to proper military usage, at 1730 hrs.

The Army uses the 24-hour clock and so avoids confusion between a.m. and p.m. When it comes to midnight the question of whether it should be 2400 hours or 0000 hours is resolved by ignoring it altogether, so that for all practical purposes the clock jumps from 2359 hours to 0001 hours.

So at 1730 hours after a mad dash following the evening meal, the guard detail parades in Best BD for inspection by the Orderly Officer. The one judged to be the best turned out is selected as what is called the "stick man." This fortunate fellow does not have to stand guard duty, but spends the night in the guard room, making tea as required, keeping the fire stoked, and snoozing between times.

Not being particularly given to "bull", I never achieved the coveted honour. I did make a special effort on one occasion, but was unsuccessful, so I never tried again. I attributed my failure at the time to the fact that the greatcoat with which I had been issued was of Second World War vintage, while the winner was wearing one of the latest design, very much smarter in cut.

As soon as the parade was over, it was back to the barracks to change into Second Best boots and BD, then off to the guard room. The six guards were paired off (generally we could choose our own partner), and lots drawn to decide the order of duty. Each pair did two shifts "on stag", each stag being of two hours with a four hour break between stags. One guard stood at the camp gate, while the other known as the "Prowler", patrolled the fence and generally roamed around the camp, or more likely found somewhere to hide! Each one did an hour on the gate, while the other was having a "skive".

The theory was that since everyone did only four hours actually on duty they could have eight hours' sleep, and so should be bright-eyed and bushy-tailed in the morning. This was not how it worked out in practice. It was impossible to get any uninterrupted sleep, what with the clatter of the guard changing every two hours, and people cursing, playing cards or brewing up, so that tempers would be pretty frayed by 0600 hours and then it was back on parade again after breakfast.

It was generally accepted that the second shift was the worst. The 2000 to 2200 hours wasn't too bad, but the 0200 to 0400 was a killer. At this hour the body mechanisms are said to be at their lowest ebb, and I would agree with that assessment. Not surprisingly, everybody hated guard duty!

At Christmas I managed to get two weeks' leave, for which I was well and truly ready! It was normal for everyone to have a fortnight off each year, the timing being of course at the Army's discretion. The Christmas-New Year period was naturally especially popular, and as the regiment was in virtual hibernation at that time of the year anyway, it was common to grant time off to as many people as could be spared, leaving only a skeleton staff. It was often the practice to give Christmas leave to the English blokes, so that the Scotsmen could be off for their main celebration at New Year.

It was wonderful to be home for a couple of weeks — I did enjoy strutting around the village in my uniform, showing off shamelessly! Already I had gained several pounds in weight in the last three months, and my civilian clothes were now a bit too snug for comfort.

All too soon the fortnight was up, and it was time for a reluctant return to Larkhill. I was struck by the phenomenon that two weeks in Cornwall was over in the blink of an eye, while a similar period on the Salisbury Plain seemed to stretch for an eternity!

The chief problem for me at Larkhill was the boring, mind-numbing lack of anything purposeful to do. Day followed day with the same depressingly monotonous regularity. I would not go as far as to say that I wished I was back at Tonfanau, though at least there we had been kept so busy that there was no time to reflect on our misery, but I did heartily wish that I was elsewhere. I was reminded of the old Cornish saying: "'e be like Farmer 'ocking's ducks, never 'appy less they be where they bain't!" I was sure that if I had to spend the next eighteen months or more in this depressing environment, I would become a basket case long before my demob date. I just disliked the place with an intensity that bordered on hatred!

But unbeknownst to me, my delivery was at hand. It could not have been because the Army had become aware of my dissatisfaction, and decided to relieve my suffering — the authorities were not that sensitive — but whatever the underlying reason might have been, like the 7th.Cavalry arriving in the nick of time to rescue a beleaguered wagon train, salvation came, in the form of orders to pack my gear and proceed to my new posting, at the 14th (Cole's Kop) Independent Locating Battery in Woolwich. No explanation was offered for the transfer — the Army does not feel obliged to justify its arbitrary decisions — "just do it!" is the only explanation deemed necessary!

5

COLE'S KOP BATTERY

The 14th. Battery. (I suspect that the honorific "Cole's Kop" related to some long- forgotten and obscure military action in the Boer War, or perhaps even the Zulu Wars, in which an Artillery unit had distinguished itself, and had thus be acknowledged), was housed in fairly ancient but nevertheless comfortable, solid multi-storey buildings consisting largely of six-man rooms. I was to find that there are some advantages in being part of an independent battery — there was a sense of being a member of a more tightly-knit group than in a fully-fledged regiment. The only drawback I could identify was that because of the smaller number of people available for guard duty, I found myself performing that most distasteful task about every five days.

The radar sets at the 14th were compact units mounted on self-propelled half- track trucks of American manufacture. Because it was still the middle of winter, and as I mentioned before, the Army has an aversion to field exercises at that time of year, I never actually saw these vehicles move.

There is in the Artillery an institution known as "stable hour", during which in earlier times was an hour a day devoted to the care of the horses used to draw the gun carriages, but which in modern times took the form of attending to the care and maintenance of the unit's vehicles. In the absence of anything else to do, the stable hour at Woolwich took up most of the morning every day except Sunday. The result was that all the vehicles at the 14th were in immaculate, show-room condition at all times!

As far as military activity was concerned, there was very little of it, apart from an occasional lecture on the theory and practice of radar operation, and the usual bit of square-bashing to relieve the monotony, very much the same as at Larkhill. But here at least there were many more sources of entertainment within easy reach. Cinemas, pubs, dancehalls and so forth were in walking distance of the barracks, so a variety of diversions were at hand as long as the necessary funds were available! The public baths were just down the road, and for a mere shilling it was possible to luxuriate in a tubful of hot water, soap and towels provided at no extra cost. Sheer bliss! The proximity of such amenities made life reasonably tolerable.

In February of that year parts of Kent were devastated by the worst floods that had been known in living memory. In the dire emergency resulting from this natural disaster, the services of the 14th. Bty were enlisted in the great task of flood relief. For several days, every morning at first light, we were taken by truck to the stricken area, where we spent all day, often knee-deep in near freezing water, filling and carrying sand bags to build a levee against the rising waters. It was exhausting work, and at the end of each day it was heavenly to have a good scrub and a hot meal, and hit the sack.

There was a good deal of cheerful camaraderie and bantering among us as the work progressed, and often someone would break out into raucous song, by way of keeping up morale. It so happened that one of our junior officers was a 2nd. Lt. by the name of Faith, and a popular song of the time was one about the ability of faith to move mountains. Inevitably then, one day when our resident baritone was treating us to a rendition of this ballad, a voice from a nearby work party bellowed "Well, let him get his ass over here and shift this bloody lot!" This sally of course drew a gale of laughter from everyone within earshot, including Lt. Faith himself. He was a good sort of bloke, and very popular with the mob.

When the flood, having been successfully contained, at length subsided, and the Thames returned to the confines of its banks, our job there was finished, and we went back to our normal routine. At the parade held in honour of the occasion, we were congratulated by our C.O. on our efforts. Only the Gunners, he asserted, could have prevailed in such a Herculean endeavour — clearly a fatuous claim of course. I feel sure that the Pioneer Corps, being far more experienced in such matters, would have done equally well. It was just that ours was the closest available unit at the time. Still, it was nice to hear a word of praise for a change! Apart from anything else, it had been a good public relations exercise from the point of view of the Army, which gained much kudos among the local citizenry as a result.

Not very long after this episode another crisis arose, one which affected me personally. One of my room-mates was a clerk in the Battery office, so we were able to keep tabs on what was happening, and what was likely to. One evening, however, he came in with some alarming news, claiming that my name was on the short list for posting to a special unit that was to be formed to represent the Royal Artillery at the parade in honour of the Coronation of Queen Elizabeth the 2nd. , scheduled to take place on the second of June, a bare four months away. Now this fellow was a bit of a joker, and he might have been having a "lend" of me. I thought that it was quite possible, because I had never been noted for being particularly smartly turned out, and it seemed odd that I should be considered for such an important ceremonial occasion. Nevertheless, the merest chance that he might be telling the truth was so horrendous as to be beyond contemplation! Imagine the "bull", the spit and polish, the meticulous drill that would be involved, It could not be countenanced at any cost!

It was not that I had anything against the monarchy — on the contrary, except for one brief "bolshie" period in my earlier youth when I was anti-everything, I considered myself a loyal subject of the Queen for whom I have always had the greatest admiration, not only as Head of State, but as a person as well. But this was different, this was a critical situation requiring drastic action, and very quickly at that!

There was nothing else for it — I had to put as much distance between myself and Westminster Abbey as possible in the shortest possible time. Like many others, I had from time to time pondered the possibility of applying for service abroad, and there were plenty of options of course, considering Britain's far-flung commitments in so many parts of the world. But the indolence and apathy engendered by life in the Army had hitherto prevented me from taking any positive action in the matter. Now, however, I had a powerful and compelling incentive.

So the next morning, as soon as the parade was dismissed, I hurried over to the Battery Orderly Room and requested a transfer application form. On the form there was a space for "Preferred Theatre of Operations." I had previously given some thought to the question, and concluded that a request for one of the more desirable postings, Jamaica or Hong Kong for example, while it might ultimately be successful, would probably take far too long because of the greater demand for such plums, and in my case time was of the essence. I reasoned therefore that the best chance of success was to go for the least attractive option.

So in the space provided I wrote in bold capitals "KOREA." I knew that there was some public disquiet about sending conscripts on active service against their will, and I thought that volunteers might therefore be welcome. My supposition proved to be accurate, for in an embarrassingly short time, a matter of a mere two or three days (a phenomenally prompt response by Army standards), my request was granted, and I was ordered to report to the transit camp just across the road from the 14th, where a draft was in the process of being assembled for imminent departure eastwards. The urgency of filling the draft was no doubt one of the reasons for my immediate transfer. Whatever the reason, I was grateful that the interminable delays so characteristic of the Army in matters of this kind were in this case completely absent.

6

IN TRANSIT

Things moved rapidly at the transit depot. One of the first things we were instructed to do was to stencil on our kitbags the letters DBDMF. The significance of the letters was not explained to us — probably it was considered that it was none of our business, but it appeared that were the code for our draft, and would be recognised by somebody somewhere.

There were people from different regiments from all over the country in the draft, and we were just getting to know each other when we were all granted a fortnight's embarkation leave. Coming so soon after my Christmas leave, this was a real bonus for me. I was determined to make the most of it, in the knowledge that this was the last I would see of Cornwall for about eighteen months.

Those two weeks were very enjoyable — I was lionised by friends and family, who seemed more concerned about my immediate future than I was. While I had some feelings of regret at the prospect of leaving everything that was familiar, there was the excitement and thrill of anticipation of the adventure about to begin.

When we all arrived back at Woolwich, life began to be a bit hectic — there was much to be done before embarkation, and time was getting short. During the time we were in transit, there was very little in the way of actual military activity — we were far too busy with the preparations for our departure. On the one serious parade that was held, we were informed that our draft was over-subscribed by three people, and so anyone who felt that he had any grounds for exclusion, for example family reasons, or any other compelling cause, was invited to take a step forward, and his case would be considered without prejudice. Not a man moved, and the parade was dismissed. How the surplus was disposed of I never discovered — presumably the supernumeraries were held over until the next draft.

The next item on the agenda was the issue of our new uniforms and equipment. Gone were the heavy serge battledress and the beetle- crusher boots with their thirteen hobnails each and their brilliant sheen. Instead we got the so-called "jungle greens", uniforms of a much lighter material and with a full-length jacket — very smart indeed! The boots had leather uppers and rubber soles — far more comfortable, though they did not make the same satisfying crashing sound as the when coming to attention!

The new webbing gear was especially pleasing. It was of slightly lighter material than the standard issue, was drab green in colour, and, glory be, did not require Blanco — all it needed was a good scrub now and then. Added to this happy state of affairs was the fact that the irksome brassware was replaced by dull black gun metal. The only items of clothing that remained the same were socks, underwear, shirts and the much-loved beret with its gleaming brass badge. The badge was the only thing left for which Brasso was required, so that a tin of it would last a long, long time.

There was one item that caused us a good deal of surprise, not to say bewilderment, and that was the issue of a set of light blue cotton pyjamas. As far as we were concerned, this was a startling departure from the norm, judging by our experience of Army life up to this point. From what we had heard the provision of such luxury items might well have been appropriate in the pampered ranks of the RAF "Brylcreem Boys." After all, they were even issued with sheets, or so it was said. But we were Army — they were supposed to be toughening us up for the rigours that were to come, yet they were treating us like human beings!

There must have been some ghastly mistake by someone at the QM, I thought, this can't last. And of course I was right. When we arrived in Japan some six weeks later, these symbols of sybaritic decadence were taken from us, and it was back to the more familiar sleepwear of singlet and drawers cellular.

In due course our little skive at the transit depot came to an end — it had been quite an enjoyable respite from the normal humdrum routine of life in a home posting. We had been well treated, the food was pretty good, as was the accommodation, and we had had more leisure time than we had expected. But now the time for departure into the unknown was at hand.

Early in the morning of the day for sailing, right after breakfast, we bade farewell to the transit depot and were taken to the railway station, where we boarded the train for Southampton. There lying at anchor awaiting our arrival was the troopship the M.V. (H.M.T.) "Empire Pride." She was a converted cargo vessel of some 9000 tons, and looked very impressive to the landlubber eyes of her prospective passengers. Later on we were to discover that her lack of stabilisers, however, was a distinct disadvantage whenever we encountered heavy seas.

7

ABOARD M.V. (H.M.T)
"EMPIRE PRIDE"

There were about 1500 troops altogether, replacements from every branch of the Army, and so embarkation was a lengthy and time-consuming business. We boarded in groups according to regiment or corps, tramping up the gangplank, kitbag over shoulder, in a scene reminiscent of the many we had seen in wartime newsreels, and were directed to our respective decks — our home for the next month and a half.

The deck space allocated to each group consisted of an area in which there were fixed tables and benches — obviously this was to be our combined living, eating and sleeping quarters. Each man was given a hammock. Few of us had ever had dealings with hammocks, and our efforts to master their use were, on that first night, hilarious. They were, we were told, to be suspended from hooks in the ceiling, or whatever a ceiling is called in nautical parlance. Seafarers have a language all their own which is largely incomprehensible to the average landsman. There is definitely an art in getting into a hammock. At the first few attempts several of our number tumbled unceremoniously out of the accursed things, and literally ' 'hit the deck."

However, when all the hammocks were slung, and finally occupied, they were so tightly packed together that it was virtually impossible to fall out of them. In any case, we soon found out that the level of comfort provided by a hammock was not conducive to restful slumber, and after the first miserable night most of us decided to abandon the unequal struggle, concluding that it would be preferable simply to roll out the hammock on the floor and sleep there. For one thing it was very cold trying to sleep in a hammock. It was now early April, and still quite cool. The cold seemed to creep up from below and freeze the bones. Apparently, so we were told, the trick is to fold one of the blankets provided to make a kind of mattress, and cover oneself with the other. But mostly we opted for sleeping on the floor, or the tables, or under the tables — anywhere where sufficient space could be found. It seemed safer, and was certainly more comfortable.

Conditions on board were very cramped , as is to be expected in a situation where the chief consideration is the accommodation of as many people as possible, the ease and comfort of the unfortunates coming a poor second. The voyage after all was not intended to be a pleasure cruise!

At mealtimes we collected the food from the galley in our mess tins and took it back to the mess deck to eat. The meals were fairly bland, consisting largely of porridge, bread and butter, boiled cod and strong tea — nothing that might have a tendency to upset fragile stomachs!

It was fair enough in the Channel, but the sea got a bit choppy in the Bay of Biscay, causing many blokes to suffer the misery of sea-sickness. I'm happy to say that I was never myself seriously affected by this curse, an occasional feeling of mild queasiness was the worst I experienced — never severe enough to cause vomiting. To be honest, it wasn't too bad in the Bay of Biscay — the weather was chilly enough, at least in the early stages, but it wasn't really stormy, and the ship didn't roll too violently. It got much worse later on in the voyage, especially in the Indian Ocean, and later still in the East China Sea.

By the time we were approaching the Straits of Gibraltar, the legendary Pillars of Hercules, it had become relatively calm, and it was quite pleasant leaning over the guardrail enjoying the picturesque view of the white-washed, red roofed cottages on the cliff tops along the Portuguese coast.

Before long we were passing through the Straits and entering the Mediterranean, the Rock on our left and the coast of North Africa on our right. As we passed Gib. some of the blokes expressed envy of the lucky blighters who would spend their two years in this cushy number, but on reflection we realised that service here would involve a high degree of "bull" in order to impress the local citizenry, while where we were headed, we felt sure, that would not be an issue since our contact with civilians would be minimal. So all things considered, we were content to continue on our merry way.

Here in the Mediterranean all was calm, the weather was warming up and the sea was as smooth as a mirror. Now it was warm enough to sleep on the top deck, so every night we carted our hammocks topside and rolled them out on the deck. It was for me the most pleasant part of the whole voyage, lying there under the stars, lulled by the throb of the engines and the swish of the waves as the ship sailed sedately at fifteen knots across the tranquil waters.

The only downside to this idyllic existence was that at 0600 hours sharp the Lascar crew would appear, and shrilly announce that they were about to "Washee, washee deck, Johnny, get up Johnny, six o' clock, Johnny, getup!" It was prudent then to get a shuffle on and clear decks before the blighters got their high-pressure hoses rolled out and switched on, or there was a danger of being washed overboard. These fellows had a keen sense of their responsibilities to their employers, and were rigid in the meticulous observance of their routine!

Having rolled and stowed our hammocks, we would get cleaned up, and proceed to the galley to grab our breakfast. After that there were the routine chores to be done, cleaning up the deck and so on. Generally there were various tasks to be allocated, more I think to keep us occupied and out of mischief than anything else. The Lascars' cleaning duties seemed to be confined to the top deck — below decks was our responsibility. One perennial job was the cleaning and polishing the brass surrounds of the portholes, which in the salt air would become tarnished within an hour or so of having been brought to a mirror finish.

Most of the day however was spent in glorious idleness, gossiping, or dozing in the warm sunshine, or leaning over the rail to watch the cavorting porpoises. These beautiful creatures would follow us for miles, leaping and splashing, diving under the ship, and generally putting on a spectacular show, almost as if they were aware of our admiration for their antics and enjoying the attention. "Their exuberance was infectious, a tonic to the spirits. There were also the flying fish. Huge schools of them would suddenly break the surface and glide in a shimmering mass for incredible distances before disappearing below the waves.

It really was a privilege to enjoy these experiences — in those austere post-war days strict currency regulations prevented people from taking large amounts of sterling out of the country even if they had it. The best most people could manage by way of holidays was a week or two at Butlins. A Mediterranean cruise was a thing of dreams, a luxury reserved for the rich and famous. Yet here I was, revelling in the warmth of the sunshine and balmy breeze, in blissful idleness, and without a care in the world, all at the expense of H.M.'s Government! Admittedly the Empire Pride was not exactly a Cunarder - the accommodation was cramped, and the food was hardly cordon bleu, but the scenery and the sunshine were the same! These were halcyon days indeed.

As we made our leisurely way eastward it was impossible not to reflect upon the chequered history of this fabled waterway. Recognised as the birthplace of democracy in the Athens of the 5th. Century B.C. it had known the rise and fall of successive empires - Egyptians, Persians, Greeks, Carthaginians — all had had their days of glory, and had faded into oblivion, until the rise of the greatest of them all, the mighty Roman Empire, whose citizens, with the unconscious arrogance and insensitivity of imperialists throughout the ages, referred to the Mediterranean as "Mare Nostrum"- Our Sea.

Among the troops aboard, were members of every regiment and corps which were then serving in Korea. These were replacements not only for casualties, but also for those whose term of enlistment was approaching its expiry date. Because so many of us were either NS men or short term regulars, the turnover of personnel was frequent. This was in contrast to the situation in WW2, for example, when enrolment was "for the duration", which meant that those who joined up together could expect to remain together for long periods. The tendency in those circumstances was to form strong and lasting bonds of friendship, to an extent that would not necessarily obtain amongst NS men, where the constant coming and going meant an ever-changing population.

The end result of all this was that there was no doubt much less of a trend towards post-service reunions. As a matter of fact, in more than half a century since my discharge from the Army,

I have not encountered a single one of the hundreds of soldiers with whom I had been acquainted during my service days.

On board the ship members of each regiment tended to stick together — this was natural enough of course, the more so because of the cramped conditions. The tendency was to form groups of two or three of similar type and having similar interests. I teamed up with a Scotsman named Kinloch — Jock of course, I never used his first name, probably never even knew it. We spent most of our time together on board, and went ashore together whenever we were in port. I was sorry that when we arrived in Korea we were posted to different units, and I never saw him again.

All too soon our little Mediterranean cruise came to an end, and we made our first landfall since leaving Southampton at Port Said. We were not allowed ashore there, because at the time there was considerable tension between the Egyptians and the British troops stationed in the Suez Canal area. This was only three or four years before the eruption of the Suez crisis and the invasion by British, French and Israeli forces following President Nasser's nationalisation of the Canal. Relations with the Egyptians were already strained almost to breaking point, to say the least of it.

So as soon as the ship had taken on water and whatever else was running short, we weighed anchor and were on our way through the Canal and into the Red Sea. As we progressed it seemed at times that the Canal was so narrow that it would be possible to climb onto the guardrail and leap ashore if anyone were misguided enough to wish to do so.

We had to endure a good deal of abuse and ridicule from Egyptian dissidents along the banks, which caused a lot of anger amongst the soldiers. This was particularly so with the detachment of the famous Black Watch, who became especially incensed at the locals' display, and at one stage these feisty Scots had to be forcibly restrained from breaking into the armoury and seizing the Lee Enfields stored there, with which they intended to wreak havoc among what they referred to as "the bloody Wogs."

At the same time we considered it was justifiable for us to jeer at the few Tommies that we saw, urging them to "get some (service) in", and enquiring what life was like in a "home posting," Another favourite was "get your knees brown" — a fatuous remark indeed, as it turned out, since these fellows were in fact wearing shorts (rather baggy, shapeless things they were too, generally known as "Bombay Bloomers"), so that their knees were already quite brown. We ourselves never had that experience, because where we were going we were never issued with shorts, it being too cold in winter and there being too many malaria-bearing mosquitoes in summer. In any case we would not have wished to change places with those blokes — at least we could expect to have the support of the local population in Korea!

We got clear of the Canal without serious incident, and entered the Red Sea, which was calm, and the weather was warm, perhaps a bit warmer than we had got used to so far. So it was pleasant enough, but I'm afraid the Med. had spoiled me, and I never got the same enjoyment out of the rest of the voyage as I had during the Mediterranean idyll.

It wasn't long before we reached our next port of call — the city of Aden on the tip of the Arabian Peninsula. Here we were allowed ashore for about four hours, a welcome break from the restricted conditions aboard the Empire Pride, despite the brevity of the respite. However I was far from impressed by Aden — it was dirty, dusty and overly hot for comfort. Moreover the natives were less than friendly and welcoming — no doubt they were well aware from previous experience that our presence was unlikely to prove profitable for them! In all I have no pleasant memories of Aden, and I was quite happy to return to the ship.

Despite the monotony of shipboard life, there were some diversions to relieve the boredom. There was a sort of lottery to forecast the distance the ship would travel each day, and this proved to be more difficult than I would have expected, because the Empire Pride, being a small vessel, was much affected by wind and tide. On one particular day in the Indian Ocean it was so stormy that we lost a fair bit of our forecast progress, and it took several days to make up the deficit.

On one of the calmer days, just to remind us that we were still in the Army, we were taken in batches to the rear deck, where we were issued with rifles. We were to loose off a few rounds each at balloons, which had been thrown overboard, and were merrily bobbing about in the ship's wake in a manner that virtually ensured their immunity.

Then there were the inoculations and vaccinations, which took place at frequent intervals. There were smallpox, T.A.B. (whatever that was), tetanus, cholera and typhus jabs, and a test to identify any allergies that might be present. Most of these required multiple injections, so that by the time they were all finished our upper arms were like the top of a pepper pot. In those days HIV/AIDS was unknown, and hepatitis was not an issue, so it was not considered necessary to replace the needles until they became so blunt that they could penetrate the skin only with great difficulty. That being the case, the trick, as I very quickly learned, was to get at the head of the queue while the needle was still sharp!

Sometimes someone would faint even before reaching the head of the line. We would shuffle along, arm akimbo, and the M.O. would administer the jab as though dealing with inanimate objects on an assembly line. As their turn got closer and closer, the prospect was too much for some people, and they would keel over. Oddly it was not only the apparently weaker blokes who succumbed in this way — just as often it would be one of the more macho types that you would expect to take it in their stride. The process was spread over several weeks because of the need for follow-up injections, and by the end of it I was convinced that we were now protected against every ailment that might afflict us, with the possible exception of fowl pest and in-growing toenails.

There was also a boxing tournament organised by the officer in charge of entertainment. Because the project aroused great interest and attracted a large number of competitors, the programme occupied a few weeks. It was designed to be an in-ter-regimental tournament, so there was huge rivalry involved. One of the middleweight contenders was a Gunner, and naturally he had enormous support from the many RA blokes on board. It turned out that he was an accomplished boxer, and he easily outpointed his opponents in the elimination bouts. He may have lacked a killer punch, but his skill was such that his tougher opponents could hardly lay a glove on him. In the final he was matched against a brawny infantryman. This fellow was more of a brawler than a boxer, and though he gave our man a lot more trouble than had any of his previous opponents, our champion emerged the clear winner on points, to the delight of every ar-tilleryman on the ship. Unfortunately, after we landed in Japan and were preparing to leave for Korea, this fellow was found to suffering from a hernia which required an operation, so that he had to be left behind. Presumably he followed at a later date, but I never saw him again.

Anyway, all these activities kept us well enough occupied,

and the time passed pleasantly. After we left Aden we ran into a lot of heavy weather in the Arabian Sea, worse than anything we had encountered in the Bay of Biscay. During the storms the Empire Pride was tossed about like a cork, causing a great deal of misery among those affected by sea-sickness. At these times I preferred to be on the top deck leaning over the rail watching the angry waves, as long as it wasn't raining of course! The fresh air was far more beneficial than the fetid conditions below, listening to the groans of my less fortunate comrades.

One day, as I was thus occupied, I was treated to a sight that gladdened my heart. There was on board an RSM, whose job seemed to be to act as a kind of liaison officer between the ship's company and the soldiery. Apparently he traveled to and fro on the ship, and so was a de facto member of the crew. He was an obnoxious person, full of his own importance, and universally detested by one and all.

On this particular day I was at my usual position at the rail when I spotted the RSM staggering up from below. His normally ruddy face had a deathly pallor, with a peculiar greenish tinge. With a groan he lurched towards the rail and proceeded to deposit his breakfast into the ocean, in a move often referred to by the unsympathetic as "feeding the fishes." Well, I thought, there is some justice after all!

At last we reached the calm waters of Colombo harbour, and no sooner had we dropped anchor than the ship was surrounded by a fleet of what we learned were known as "bum boats." Without preamble the native occupants of these fragile- looking craft launched into their sales pitch, offering a wide range of goods at what they claimed were rock bottom prices. Their wares included everything from bananas and pineapples (which we had been warned by our superiors not to touch for health reasons) to what purported to be genuine Rolex Oyster watches, but which were in fact cheap and unreliable imitations. One or two of the more respectable vendors were allowed aboard, and they did a fair bit of business, especially in the line of souvenirs, as what they had to offer could be minutely scrutinised before any money changed hands.

Far more diverting were the youngsters on the boats, who would dive to retrieve coins (mostly sixpences of course, with perhaps the occasional shilling), tossed overboard by the cheering spectators. These lads would grab the coins before they sank, and when they had a mouthful, would spit them into their boat and dive again for another batch. Only when the offerings were coppers would they once in a while decline to make the effort at retrieval.

Shore leave in Colombo was much more interesting than in Aden. Jock and I spent an hour or two wandering around the city, and paid a visit to a beautiful park in which there was a very imposing statue of Queen Victoria, as well as a variety of glorious plants and flowers, most of which were unfamiliar to us.

At one stage during our perambulations around the park we were accosted by a sleazy-looking character, who tried to sell us what I supposed was probably marijuana. This we angrily rejected, offering him in turn a kick in the backside if he didn't make himself scarce without delay. At this time neither of us had any knowledge of drugs of any kind, except tobacco and alcohol. Drug-taking was extremely rare in the British Army; at least I never encountered any instances of it during my service.

Walking around the streets we noticed that at various locations there were lengths of thick rope hanging from brackets on the walls. The ends of these ropes were smouldering, and we observed people using them to light their cigarettes. This novel idea seemed eminently sensible and practical, as during the rainy season frequent heavy downpours had a tendency to make matches soggy and difficult to light. A commendable example, I thought, of ingenuity on the part of the city elders.

Every city has its share of light-fingered street urchins — Colombo was no exception. I had just lit a cigarette, and was gazing into a shop window deciding whether to go in and have a haggling session with the owner, or keep my money in my pocket, when I became aware of a movement behind me. Looking around, I realised that my cigarette had been plucked from between my fingers and a barefoot gamin was haring up the street with it. I hadn't felt a thing. When the little rascal reached the corner, he turned and with a wide grin waved the cigarette before disappearing out of sight. Cheeky little sod.

Our next port of call was Singapore, which we found was well on the way to recovery from the ravages of the Japanese. There were many beautiful and interesting sights to see, and everything seemed to be much cleaner and tidier that what we had seen in Aden or Colombo. It was a great pity that constraints of time and money made it impossible to take full advantage of the opportunity for a more thorough investigation, especially as there was no shortage of guides to point out particular places of interest.

It was the policy of the authorities to make only a small allowance available for shore leave purposes, in order to minimise the chance of any of us absconding in the wake of a drunken orgy, and failing to return to the ship. In fact, we did lose one of our number in this way; it seemed that one of the infantrymen had disappeared, and we had to sail without him. I have no doubt that he would have been apprehended by the MPs before long, and I expect that he would then have spent a very uncomfortable spell in detention before rejoining his regiment. The Army does not take a sympathetic view of desertion.

Almost before we realised it, our stay in Singapore was over, and we were heading north-east to our next destination, which was Hong Kong, the Pearl of the Orient. During the passage through the South China Sea we struck some pretty heavy weather, and at one stage I was horrified at the sight of a Chinese junk with several people aboard being tossed about alarmingly. Surely, I thought, they will never reach land! None of our crew seemed to be at all concerned — apparently these craft, despite their fragile appearance, were eminently seaworthy, as they had proved over a period of several centuries.

We arrived in Hong Kong in the middle of the day, and after lunch and the usual clean-up operations, we were given shore leave for a few hours. We had heard from one of the old hands that "Hong Kong" means Fragrant Harbour, but at first we were unable to detect any evidence that the name was an appropriate one. The harbour seemed to be chock full of sampans, on which families appeared to live. The conditions must have been uncomfortable as well as unsanitary I should think, and those on the outlying boats would have to clamber over several others to reach land. I shuddered to think what the chaos would be if a typhoon struck the place.

As usual Jock and I went ashore together, and as we wandered around the streets, which were narrow and crowded — the place was like a honeycomb — we inevitably became hopelessly lost. We weren't worried though — we were fascinated by the unfamiliar sights, sounds and smells surrounding us, and were confident that we would be able to get directions back to the ship from somebody.

The streets were packed with narrow little shops, whose owners stood at the entrance trying to entice prospective customers inside. Jock's eye was taken by some trinket or other that he was determined to have, and with the canniness characteristic of his race, entered into a haggling session with the shopkeeper. The negotiations became very heated, and this resulted in a gathering of Chinese onlookers. As the dispute continued we were surrounded by a large, noisy, gesticulating mob, without a friendly face to be seen. Because we had strayed from the main thoroughfares into the backstreets, there were no other soldiers in sight, and I became very uneasy at our isolation. With difficulty I finally convinced Jock that we would be far better off away from there, and we started to move back the way we had come, trying as best we could to maintain an air of nonchalance. As we retreated the crowd parted to let us through, and closed behind us. No hostile move was made against us, but the atmosphere was decidedly menacing. Anyway after a few minutes the crowd lost interest and much to our relief seemed to melt away. Jock was more sanguine about the whole business than I felt, but it is true to say that I had been more than a little nervous!

There were of course many bargains to be had in HK but as usual the shortage of funds was a limiting factor, and in any case there didn't seem to be much point in burdening ourselves with a lot of knick-knacks that we could more conveniently pick up on the return journey.

We finally made our way back to the ship without further incident, and reflected that our experience of HK had been both interesting and exciting. In fact the whole voyage, despite the often uncomfortable conditions, had been nothing short of a revelation to a young, naive country boy like me — an experience that I would never have aspired to in civilian life.

Now our cruise came to an end — the holiday was over, and on our arrival at the transit camp in Kure, on the Japanese island of Honshu, we were soon reminded that we were still in the Army! We were now issued with our own personal rifle and bayonet, which we were warned must be seen as our most prized possessions, and jealously guarded at all times.

One of the first jobs we had in Kure was to "zero in" our rifles, (never to be referred to as ' 'guns"-guns were 25-pounder cannon, a different thing altogether!). The process of zeroing in consisted of firing five shots at a target on the rifle range, and then taking the target to the armourer for examination of the result. If the rifle was found to be firing, for example, high, or to the right, or whatever, the expert would make minute adjustments to the sights, and the rifleman would go back to the range and have another try. This carried on until a satisfactory standard of accuracy was achieved.

It so happened that the range was laid out in such a way that the butts were at a somewhat lower level than the firing positions. This meant that you were actually firing downhill, as it were. At this time I was very lean, and at this angle the brass butt plate recoiled painfully against my bony shoulder. I was relieved therefore when it was found that the sight adjustment after my first effort had been successful, and my second go was near enough to pass muster.

Apart from this, and a bit of a route march now and then to keep us in shape, the greater part of our five days in Kure was taken up with lectures on a variety of subjects. There were a couple of films about the dangers of liaisons with ladies of the night. There was a British-made film which showed in graphic detail the horrific results of contracting syphilis. There was also an American film which was, (uncharacteristically perhaps) rather more subtle, and therefore probably more effective. It told the story of a G.I. returning home after WW2. He was infected with V D, and inevitably passed on the disease to his wife, with devastating results to their marriage. Not totally convinced that these cautionary tales would be a foolproof deterrent, the M.O. conducted frequent examinations to be on the safe side!

There were several lectures to boost morale, and to give us some idea of what lay ahead. For a couple of years there had been a series of talks between the UN top brass and the Chinese authorities with a view to arranging a cease-fire and eventual peace treaty, since hostilities had reached a stalemate with no conclusion in sight. At times, we were told, the two sides had seemed to be on the verge of agreement, then some technicality would arise, and it was back to square one. We were told therefore to ignore any rumours (always good advice in the Army anyway!), as there had been many false starts up till now.

We were given some insight into the composition and organisation of the First Commonwealth Division, which we would be joining. The division comprised three brigades, the 25th, the 28th and the 29th.

The 25th was composed mainly of Canadian troops, one infantry battalion each of the Royal Canadian Regiment (RCR), the Princess Patricia's Canadian Light Infantry (PPCLI), and a French-Canadian regiment, the Royal 22nd, familiarly known as the Van Doos, from the French vingt- deuxieme (French for twenty-second). They were also sometimes referred to rather unkindly as the "Lamplighters", in reference to their supposed predilection for the use of phosphorous flares to illuminate the battlefield when under attack.

There was also the 81st Field Regt. RCA and a squadron of the Lord Strathcona's Horse. Like the British, the Canadians also favoured colourful names for their units! They had various support troops, Ordnance, Service Corps and so on.

The 28th, the Commonwealth Brigade, had two battalions of the Royal Australian Regiment, plus a British battalion, supported by the 16th Field Regiment, RNZA, together with all the usual ancillaries. We naturally had more affinity with the New Zealanders, since they were fellow Artillerymen. They were a cheeky mob, not averse to a bit of good-natured boasting. Their most outrageous claim was that their Gunners had achieved such a high degree of accuracy that they had developed an economical method of disposing of enemy bunkers. Their practice, they said, was to load the first three of a Troop's guns with wooden shells, and the fourth with a normal high explosive one. The first three would be fired rapidly, and the fourth after a short interval. The wooden shells would hit the heavily reinforced bunker door, rat-tat-tat, and when the Chinese opened up to see who was knocking, the H.E. shell would enter and annihilate the whole place.

The 29th was a completely British brigade, comprising a battalion each of the Black Watch, the Durham Light Infantry, and the Duke of Wellington's Regiment, the 42nd Field Regiment RA, a tank regiment and other support troops.

It was impossible to absorb all this information at one time, but I was to learn more about the 1st Comwel Division, and indeed about the whole of the U.N. "Police Action" force, which was collectively under the command of the U.S. Eighth Army, in the weeks following our arrival in Korea.

8

LAND OF THE MORNING CALM

As we boarded the Empire pride for the last leg of our journey, the short hop from Kure to Pusan on the southernmost tip of the Korea peninsula, we were still unaware of which unit we would be joining. It was easy enough for the infantry — they would naturally go to one or other of the companies of their battalion. But for us Gunners there were a number of possibilities, since there were two regiments, an independent battery, and various odds and sods to which we might be assigned. Besides the 42nd Field, already mentioned, there was the Light Regiment, equipped with 4.2 inch mortars, and the 74th Medium Battery, with their heavier guns. These last two units were used wherever they were needed along the divisional front.

We were told that we would be assigned to our new postings when we landed in Pusan. Perhaps the secrecy was all part of the Army's usual bloody-mindedness, or it may have been that no one was sure what the precise requirements of each unit might be from day to day.

During the short trip to Pusan I got into conversation with a young Chinese- American in a neat G.I. uniform, who was as it were "hitching a lift" back to Korea after a spot of leave in Japan. He was an interpreter with U .S. Intelligence, and his job was to interrogate Chinese P.O.W's and translate captured documents. He was very interesting to talk to, though of course discreet, since much of his work was hush- hush. He was friendly and courteous, not at all the type you would expect to find on the staff at Abu Ghraib or Guantanamo Bay! It did occur to me that his very presence as a casual passenger on a British troopship was an encouraging sign of co-operation and lack of formality between the allies.

On arrival in Pusan, we were treated to an impromptu welcoming concert of popular tunes performed by a U.S. Army band, who were all of African descent. They played with great verve and enthusiasm, performing some of the numbers at the trot up and down the quayside.

Then began the process of disembarkation. The exercise was performed in accordance with the Army principle commonly known as "hurry and wait", in which there is a period of confused, frenetic activity, conducted by harassed officers with clipboards, pencils and worried expressions, desperately trying to create order out of chaos. Incredibly they somehow managed to achieve their purpose, and organised the 1500 bemused troops into their appropriate groupings.

All the Artillery contingent was gathered together, and at last we discovered our next destinations. I was disappointed to find myself separated from my travelling companion, Jock Kinloch. He was to join the 61st while I was assigned to the Counter-Bombardment Troop. I learned that this was an independent troop, loosely attached to Headquarters Royal Artillery — "attached for rations" as the saying went.

There were two others going to C.B. Tp. with me; one was a bloke called Peter Cornford, who came from the town of Battle, in Sussex. This town, he proudly told me, was the actual site of the Battle of Hastings, Hastings itself being several miles away. Pete was a quiet, steady sort of fellow, easy to get along with. The other was from near Swindon in Wiltshire. His name was Brian Mace, and it transpired that he was something of an artist. He later showed me photographs of some of his paintings, which even to my untrained eye looked very good. Brian was a rather shy, retiring type, but a very nice chap when you got to know him, and the three of us became firm friends over the next year or so.

The "hurry" part of the process satisfactorily completed, the "wait" now began. This lasted at least two hours, perhaps closer to three, during which we lazed about on the beach, swapping yarns and enjoying the pleasant sunshine as we waited for the trucks that would take us to the railway station.

Trucks came and went, taking people away in groups in what turned out to be a fairly orderly fashion after all. Finally it was our group's turn, so we gathered up our belongings and boarded the truck. We were of course heavily burdened with all our equipment, including rifles, and for the first time a bandolier holding fifty rounds of ammunition, and so there was a limit to the number of bodies that could be accommodated in each truckload.

On arrival at the station we were herded onto a ramshackle-looking conveyance of uncertain vintage, and took our places on the hard wooden bench seats. Comfort was obviously not a priority on the Korean railways — the G.W .R. it was definitely not! The seating arrangements were adequate perhaps for short trips, but for the protracted journey we were to endure, with its many halts and lengthy delays when we were shunted into sidings for periods of varying duration, presumably to give way to more urgent traffic, the experience was somewhat tiresome. Sleep was at best fitful and intermittent, so we were all stiff, exhausted and decidedly cranky by the time we reached our destination.

On one of the stops along the way we were drawn up alongside a train loaded with American troops — our first encounter with our allies. We were able to get acquainted with them through the open window, as the trains were close to each other. One of them claimed to be only sixteen years old, and said he had falsified his age in order to enlist. He looked older than his years right enough, but his assertion was verified by one of his companions, who knew him in civilian life. Talk about gung- ho! Actually this was an unusual occurrence — the great majority of G.I.s were at least a couple of years older than their British counterparts, certainly among the conscripts in any case, because the call-up age in the USA was twenty, as opposed to eighteen in Britain. In fact the British troops were probably, on average, the youngest in the UN forces.

Part of the journey took place in the hours of darkness, and there were no lights on the train. We were told to be careful lighting cigarettes, for fear of attracting sniper fire (not very likely of course, but you can't be too careful!).

At last the ordeal was over, and we reached the railhead, whence we would proceed to our final destination by road. There were a number of trucks from the various units, waiting to pick up their allocation of newcomers. As there were only three of us for CB Troop, they had sent a small, 15-cwt. truck for us, while most of the other vehicles were 3-tonners.

With Fred Blinman, B. Evans and Bill Budd
prior to embarkation, April 1953

L to R, Name unkown, Kim Ki Ha, Kim On Ha (Civilian workers at CB Troop)

Scenery near CB Troop

Geordie, Devon, Brum, Self and Bob Walker with NAAFI truck at CB Troop

U.S. Army Engineers camp near CB TP. Camp

Frank Gommka Chicago Ill. Air Ground Liason Team
near CB TP. Camp Korea 1953

Wayne Messick

Your Buddy,
Wayne

WAYNE MESSICK
A GOOD FRIEND
(AT NEARBY
AIR- GROUND LIAISON
UNIT U.S ARMY)

Back of photo

Imjin River Korea 1953

New Other Rank's Mess 1954

Brian Avery

Alex McKay and Dave Whitehead

Derek Roxby (London) CB Troop 1953

Pete Cornford

Chinese Ex POW's Heading for Formosa (Now Taiwan) To join
Chiang Kai-Shek rather than return to mainland China

View from CATC Yong Dong Po Korea January 1954

C.A.T.C. (Commonwealth Artillery Training Centre)

25 Pounder Guns at C.A.T.C. 1954

Wayne Messick U.S. Signal Corps (in his USO performing costume)

28th Division ROKA
(South Korean Army) Camp

28th Division ROKA (South Korean Army) Camp

Local Korean people and typical dwellings

C.B. Troop during monsoon rainstorm 1954

Last Photo before leaving C.B. Troop

With Wayne Messick, September 1953 at
1st Comwel Div Air Ground Liason – Korea

38th Parallel in Korea

Transit camp in Kure (Japan)

Hong Kong Harbour 1954

Hong Kong Harbour 1954

Singapore streets 1954

NAAFI club (Singapore) 1954

Singapore streets 1954

Ox Cart Colombo 1954

Dave Whitehead (Brum) Colombo 1954

Author with Dave Whitehead
outside a temple in Colombo

Colombo Harbour 1954

Korean War medal, UN Medal

9

CB TROOP

When we arrived at the camp which was to be our new home, we were directed to one of the twelve-man squad tents, where there were a few empty bed spaces, vacated no doubt by the lucky ones on their way home. We introduced ourselves to our new comrades, and set about getting as well organised as conditions allowed. The tent floor was of well-trodden earth, and the furniture consisted of a variety of make-shift cots, and wooden crates for use as lockers. I settled for a spot in the corner of the tent, where the bed consisted of a duckboard supported by a couple of ammunition boxes. There was no mattress or pillow, but I was able to rectify the deficiency by folding one of my blankets double to serve as a mattress, while a folded shirt made a pillow of sorts. By shuffling about until one hip was settled into a gap in the duckboard, I managed to get comfortable enough to get to sleep — no doubt sheer fatigue helped! The following morning the other new arrivals and I were able to acquaint ourselves with the layout of the camp, and learn where everything was. The camp was situated high on the bank of the Imjin River, and consisted of half a dozen squad tents and a few smaller ones dotted about the hillside.

About a mattress; I was advised by one of the "old hands" to go and see the R.E.M.E. corporal who was in charge of the Light Aid Detachment, and was responsible for the maintenance and repair of the Troop's jeeps and trucks. He worked from a canvas tent arrangement filled with tools and spare parts of every description, a veritable cornucopia! I introduced myself and explained my problem. I found him to be a pleasant and friendly bloke, devoid of any of the self-importance that is sometimes a feature of N.C.O.s. He fossicked about in his workshop, and produced a rather worn and dilapidated engine cover. This was a canvas-covered quilted kind of blanket designed to be placed over the truck engine while it was still warm, and so prevent it from freezing solid overnight and damaging the engine block. Since it would not now be required for many months, and was in any case much the worse for wear, he was quite happy to be rid of it. This was just what I needed, so I gratefully took this lifesaver back to the tent, and thereafter slept in blissful comfort.

Tragically, not long after this episode, the corporal was killed, not by enemy action, but by a freak accident. It happened while he was a passenger in a 15cwt. truck on a road test following repairs. Apparently he was standing on the seat with his head and shoulders through the skylight in the roof when the vehicle was run off the road by a truck filled with Turkish soldiers. He died as the 15cwt. forced to swerve to avoid a head-on collision, rolled into the monsoon ditch and overturned. The driver, though badly bruised and shaken, survived.

A few weeks later I was by sheer coincidence involved in a very similar incident, though one with a happier outcome. A good friend of mine, Dave Sargeant, was the driver of the Troop's water truck, a Bedford 15cwt. fitted with a large water tank which had to be filled daily at the purification plant beside the Imjin River, and brought back for distribution to various points in the camp, there being no water supply in the camp itself. Most of the water was used in the kitchens — there were three of these, the Officers' Mess, the Sergeants' Mess, and the O.R.s' Mess. There was also a primitive shower arrangement, and a number of canvas water bags at various locations around the camp.

One day, being at a loose end, that is to say not having been allocated any specific jobs, I decided to have a skive for a few hours, and go with Dave on a bit of an outing, confident that I would not be missed. Dave was not under any strict time constraints, because there was often a queue at the purification plant, and there was no telling how much of a delay there might be. So off we went, and before taking on our load of water, we decided to shoot down to the NAAFI roadhouse, which lay some fifteen miles to the south, close to Division HQ.

There were a number of facilities at the roadhouse that were lacking at CB Troop, such as a well-equipped canteen where we enjoyed a cup of tea and a wad, then had a few games of darts, until we thought we had better be getting back — it isn't wise to overdo things, and we had spent at least an hour and a half on our little skive.

The rule of the road in Korea, as in most of the world, was that traffic drove on the right-hand side. This was awkward enough for our drivers, since all our vehicles except for the ubiquitous U.S.-made jeeps were designed to be driven on the left side of the road. Our boys soon got used to it of course, but when you were confronted by a larger vehicle approaching at high speed in the middle of the road, with its driver having scant knowledge of the Highway Code, or concern for it either, then the matter became more complicated. And that is what happened to us.

A truckload of Turks, probably en route to their rest camp, was bearing down upon us with reckless abandon. With lightning swift reflexes and quick evasive action, Dave narrowly avoided a head-on collision, at the same time somehow managing to keep the truck on the road. But it was a near thing — as it was we felt and heard a bump at the moment of contact, and then the Turks' truck roared off down the road, and was soon lost in a cloud of dust. I caught a quick glimpse of the occupants and saw from those who were not wearing helmets that their hair was close shaven, while by way of compensation they wore luxuriant moustaches. This style is apparently a cultural thing with them — a sign of masculinity or something. They certainly looked a ferocious mob.

The Turkish Brigade, some 6000 strong, held the positions immediately to the left of our sector. They formed part of the U .S. 25th Infantry Division, nicknamed the Tropic Lightning Division from their shoulder flash, which is a gold-rimmed red oak leaf with a gold lightning flash. I heard later that: like the French Foreign Legion, the 25th were never stationed in their home country, though I had no confirmation that that was true. The division later served in Vietnam, and suffered heavy casualties in the Cu Chi area, notorious for the tunnel warfare there.

The Turks had a reputation for being fierce fighters, superb infantrymen much feared by the enemy and respected by all. At a later date I had the opportunity to talk to a Turk who spoke passable English. He was very complimentary about the Commonwealth troops, and I was able to assure him that we always felt that our left flank was secure. I did not add that while his countrymen were recognised as fine infantrymen, they really ought not to be trusted with motor vehicles!

Once we had regained our composure, Dave and I became aware of a strong smell of petrol filling the cab, so we got out to see what the trouble was. We discovered that the bang we had heard as the trucks passed each other had been caused by our petrol tank being badly damaged. The cylindrical tank on the 1 5cwt. is mounted on the left side of the vehicle, and ours now had a large dent in it, having been struck, I believe, by the running board of the Turks' truck. There was also a crack from which petrol was dripping in a steady drip. This was serious — we feared that if the engine were started, the whole thing would go up in flames.

It so happened that I had bought some chewing gum at the roadhouse, and had a good mouthful of it at the time. So I took the wad and with my thumb pressed it into the rupture in the tank. As the petrol was evaporating, of course, it became very cold, and the drop in temperature caused the gum to harden and effectively block the hole in the tank. We were thus able to limp back to the water point, pick up the load of water, and return to camp. Poor old Dave had some explaining to do — my own involvement had to be kept quiet as I had been an illegal passenger! In the end the matter went no further.

Our camp was completely under canvas — the only substantial structure was the Command Post, which was a bunker dug into the side of a hill. The roof was of heavy timbers covered in sandbags, and part of the entrance was taken up by a covered truck backed up to it. The truck provided an office for the Counter Bombardment Officer on duty.

The CP was operational 24 hours a day, the officers and staff working in 12 hour shifts. The officer in charge was usually a captain, but sometimes a lieutenant. The main section of the bunker was fitted out with map tables and benches, and there were radio sets and telephones all over the place. Lighting was provided by camping-style Tilley paraffin lamps. There was a little pump on the fuel tank by which the oil was pressurised and the resultant vapour forced onto a mantle like that of a gaslight. The pump had to be operated periodically to maintain the pressure. The lamps were very efficient, giving off a brilliant white light.

Our tents were provided with the same kind of lamps, there being no electricity supply in the camp. Since transistor radios were at this time a thing of the future, the only entertainment we had was from the Tannoy system operated spasmodically by the duty clerk in the Troop office. Sometimes there was a music request segment in the programme, and once in a while there was a bit of a news bulletin. Of course, in accordance with military protocol, we were told only what it was considered appropriate for us to know.

At the time there were no U.K. newspapers available — the only paper we could get was the "Pacific Stars and Stripes", an American news sheet. This paper was of limited interest to us, since it dealt in the main with U.S. domestic news, and the latest baseball results, which of course meant little to us. Few of us knew the difference between the New York Yankees and the Boston Redsox, and cared even less!

It was not until much later on, after the truce was signed, and some semblance of sanity restored, we were able to get from the visiting NAAFI truck copies of the popular "Daily Mirror". These were bound in weekly issues, and were good value despite being a few weeks out of date. At least we could keep up with the doings of Useless Eustace, the acid comments of the editors, who called themselves the "Old Codgers", and the weekly diatribes of columnist Cassandra. He was once sued by Liberace, whose sexuality he had called into question.

Not everybody bought the paper each week of course — generally one bloke in the tent would get it, and when he had devoured it page by page would pass it around to the others. In this way everybody took a turn at footing the expense.

At the time of my arrival at CB Troop the staff required to man the Command post was at full strength, so I was assigned to general duties and became in Army parlance a GD wallah. In this role I had a variety of duties, which included maintenance of the camp's perimeter fence, and our defensive trenches around the tents. These trenches served double duty as monsoon ditches to prevent flooding of the tents during the rainy season. There were of course many other tasks of maintenance and repair around the camp, but nothing of a very onerous nature. In fact a GD wallah had a fairly easy time of it all round — it was a bit of a skive really, especially since, in stark contrast to the situation in a home posting, I didn't actually have to do any work myself. Instead I had under my supervision a couple of young Korean labourers.

There were about fifteen Korean civilian workers at CB Troop, most of whom worked in the kitchens. There was one bloke, older than the others, who was the camp barber. He charged a shilling a time, and did a pretty good job. He also took care of our laundry at a very reasonable cost.

The two workers I had for most of the time I was on GD were named Kim Ki Ha and Kim On Ha. I think they were probably brothers or cousins — there was certainly a strong family re- semblance. They were pleasant and intelligent fellows, about my age. I gathered that but for the war they would have been at university — I hoped that when peace returned they might be able to resume their studies. Ki Ha in particular had a good command of the English language, and we had many interesting conversations.

In Korean custom, as is common in Asian cultures, the surname comes first, followed by given names. This seems eminently sensible to me, considering that a baby becomes a member of the family at the moment of birth, and only acquires given names at the subsequent naming ceremony.

Similar to Smith in the English-speaking world, Kim is a very common family name in Korean — none other than the president of North Korea himself was Kim Il Sung! By contrast, the South Korean president, having been educated in the USA, styled himself Syngman Rhee, in the Western fashion.

During the time we were working together, Kim Ki Ha and I became as close as our situation permitted. Perhaps it is an exaggeration to say we were friends in the usual sense, but there was certainly a liking and respect between us. The Korean equivalent to our Mr. is the suffix —shi attached to the surname, corresponding to the Japanese —san. So to the amusement of the Koreans and the bemusement of my countrymen, Ki Ha and I took to addressing each other as Kimshi and Jenkishi (Jenkinshi was a bit too difficult to pronounce!).

I think it would be true to say that the attitude of the average British soldier towards the Koreans was one of tolerance with a touch of condescension. While there was very little in the way of open hostility, neither was there any real attempt at understanding. It is normal in wartime for the enemy to be given derogatory nicknames — the Korean War was no exception. The Chinese were referred to as "Chinks" or "Chinkies", while the Koreans (North and South) were called "Gooks." I never much liked the practice, but I suppose it was a way of demonising the enemy, so that the guilt would be minimised when you had to shoot them!

Perhaps because at the beginning I was working more closely with the Koreans than most of the blokes were at the time, I had more opportunity to get to know them. I even made an attempt to learn something of the language, though with very limited success. Apparently Korean bears no relation or resemblance to any other known language, oriental or otherwise. It was almost lost during the long and brutal Japanese occupation of the country, which they called Chosen. At that time it was forbidden to use the Korean language in schools, and all books were destroyed and replaced by Japanese texts, in an attempt to eradicate all trace of the local culture. The tragedy was averted only by Japan's defeat in 1945.

My budding relationship with Kimshi was jeopardised by a very unfortunate incident before it had had a chance to blossom. We had been given the job of cutting a 44-gallon drum in half, lengthwise, so that the halves could be mounted on stands for use as wash troughs in the Officers' Mess kitchen. This had to be done using a hammer and chisel, since the drum had been used for petrol, and the application of an oxy set would have been dangerous, even if there had been one available for us in the first place.

Petrol drums are made of heavy grade steel and are therefore very difficult to cut with hand tools, especially as when the cutting was finished, the rough edges would have to be turned down and hammered flat so as to prevent future injuries. So the operation was going to involve considerable time and effort. However dauntless Kimshi set to with a will, and as it was a warm day in early summer, the sweat was soon flowing. When he had cut one side of the drum, I called a halt, and we sat in the shade for a smoke. After a while, I told him to stay where he was - I would have a go at the cutting, thinking that a spell of physical exertion would do me no harm.

Everything was going along nicely, until the sudden appearance of the Sergeant-Major. The BSM, like so many of his contemporaries, had obviously been raised in the traditions of the British Raj, and the sight of a Briton working hard, while a "Wog", or in this case a "Gook", was sitting idly in the shade, enraged him to the point of near-apoplexy. He roared at Kimshi, and when I tried to explain that I had told Kimshi to have a spell, and that the poor bloke had been working like a Trojan, he rounded on me and threatened to charge me with insubordination. There was clearly no point in trying to reason with him while he was in this mood, so I had to let the matter rest.

I handed the tools back to Kimshi, who resumed hammering, though with less enthusiasm now, and the BSM, satisfied that the divine order of things had been restored, left the scene without another word.

Kimshi was visibly upset by the incident, for he had of course "lost face" always a serious matter in Oriental culture, and insofar as he had been acting on my instructions, in his eyes I was to blame. I tried to convince him that there was nothing I could have done in the face of superior authority, but it took several days to repair the damage that the BSM's arrogance and stupidity had caused.

Shortly after the petrol drum incident, my relationship with Kimshi was again put to the test. Sometime about the middle of June the South Korean president Syngman Rhee, recalcitrant as ever, took it upon himself to release several thousand North Korean POW's behind our lines.

It was not clear what prompted Rhee to take this extraordinary step — he must have known that it would enrage the UN authorities, and especially the Americans, who were already bearing the brunt of the international effort to prevent his country from being overrun by the red hordes. They were about the only friends he had left in the world as it was, and they were becoming disenchanted with his autocratic style, and his Luke-warm attitude towards the terms of the proposed peace negotiations, which would leave Korea much as it had been before the outbreak of hostilities. He would no doubt have been happier if Macarthur's grand plan had been allowed to proceed — to drive the Chinese out of Korea once and for all, and even carry the conflict into China itself, using whatever measures were necessary, nuclear weapons included. In that event Rhee would have been able to establish his despotic rule over the whole of a united Korea. The fact that such an action would very likely have precipitated the Third World War did not seem to figure very highly in his calculations.

Anyway, the damage was done. The security implications were obvious and enormous — it would not take many dissidents among the released POW's to wreak havoc upon the UN lines of communication and supply, so our people were understandably nervous. One of the measures adopted to ease the threat was the decision to have all the Korean civilians employed in units of the UN forces screened, and issued with new identification papers, so as to minimise the risk of infiltration by hostiles.

In our case at CB Troop, and probably most others as well, this seemed a rather pointless exercise, since all our Koreans had been with us for a long time, and were well known to everybody, at least by sight. But, as the saying goes, orders is orders, and discussion is not an option. Anyway, when our turn came it was thought that it would be no more than of nuisance value.

On the appointed day I was enjoying a smoke in the tent, in the interval between breakfast and the morning parade. Unlike those in home postings, which were occasions for minute inspection of turnout and deportment, our parades were informal affairs, the main purpose of which was to allocate duties for the day, and to issue the daily Paludrine tablet. During the warmer months we were often plagued by swarms of malaria-bearing mosquitoes. The tablets we received were so effective in preventing infection that it was considered a chargeable offence to contract malaria — it was classed as a "self-inflicted injury", in much the same way as suffering severe sunburn, or the more serious matter of shooting one's toe off.

Paludrine tablets were very small, and it was possible to swallow them without water. Also available were concentrated salt tablets, designed to prevent heat exhaustion, which in the humid conditions could be very distressing. Salt tablets were much larger, and difficult to swallow dry. However, although not compulsory, it was advisable to take one at least occasionally.

Well, as I was saying, I was enjoying a pre-parade smoke, when the bombardier poked his head through the tent flap and announced that the C.O. wanted to see me on the parade ground on the double. What now, I thought, trying to remember any possible transgression I may have committed in the recent past. Finding none, I hastened to the parade ground, filled with curiosity, and saw that there was a truck parked there, with the C.O. and a few other people standing about looking rather anxious. At the other end of the parade ground, about fifty yards away, was the group of Koreans, sitting on the ground.

The parade ground itself was not the neat and tidy tarmac square familiar to soldiers in more established stations, but was simply a piece of ground roughly levelled with the gravelly soil bulldozed into a bank at one end, along the top of which ran the road out of the camp. It was against this bank that the Koreans were leaning.

The C.O. explained that some bright spark, as yet unidentified, had started a rumour among the Koreans that the trip they were about to take was a ruse — on arrival at H.Q. they were to be handed over to the Korean authorities for recruitment into the Army of the Republic of Korea. Fearful of such a dreadful prospect, for the ROKA was well known for its harsh discipline, our civilians were refusing to have anything to do with it.

A difficult situation had therefore arisen — time was of the essence, for H.Q. had a large number or people to process, and the absence or even late arrival of a group would disrupt the smooth running of the operation, and cause a deal of resentment. Knowing that I had developed some kind of rapport with the Koreans, the C.O. wondered if I thought I could persuade them to co-operate. He was of course aware that an attempt to compel their compliance by main force would result in a nasty incident. I replied that I was willing to give it a try, as long as I knew that the rumour was false, as I did not wish to be a party to any deception.

Satisfied by the C.O.'s assurance that the object of the exercise was indeed simply the issue of new identity papers, I made my way over to where the Koreans were sitting. They were in a very sullen mood, and avoided my gaze.

I looked directly at Kimshi, and said "What's the matter, Kimshi?" to which he replied "We not go in army, Jenkishi." Looking at him steadily, I said clearly "No army, Kimshi — this is just for new picture and pass, then straight back here this afternoon." He held my gaze for a long moment, then said "Is true, Jenkishi?" "It's true, Kimshi — no army." Again that unnerving, unblinking stare. It seemed to last for an age, but must have been no more than half a minute. Then abruptly Kimshi rose, said something to the others in Korean, and headed for the truck. To my intense relief the rest of them followed suit, and the crisis was over. The C.O. was also clearly relieved, and congratulated me on a job well done. It was nice to have gained a few Brownie points, but my main satisfaction came from the knowledge that I still had the Koreans' trust.

Coronation Day, the 2nd. Of June, 1953, was celebrated at C.B. Troop with much less pomp and circumstance than I might have had to endure had I not made my timely escape from Britain. Early on the morning of the big day those of us who were not on essential duty assembled at the top of the hill overlooking the camp. From there we had a good view of the red, white and blue smoke shells from our 25- pounders bursting defiantly over the enemy positions. The surrounding hills echoed and re-echoed with our enthusiastic cheers, and we flung our berets into the air as the barrage ended.

There is no record of what the Chinese made of our frivolous pyrotechnical extravaganza — they probably saw it as yet another vulgar display of capitalist- imperialist decadence, but it did our patriotic hearts well and was a great morale- booster.

In fact, at this time at C.B. Tp. Morale was pretty high anyway, as I think it was throughout the Comwel Division. Our spirits remained high, despite our virtual isolation from the world at large — often we had no clear picture of what was happening over the next hill! There was a surprisingly high degree of harmony among the personnel. Of course there were frustrations — we naturally missed the company of girls of our age, and we also missed seeing children and old people. It could become depressing at times in the all-male environment, but still there was very little friction. There was the occasional spat, born of boredom and frustration, but it seldom went beyond verbal abuse and perhaps a bit of pushing and shoving, but actual bouts of fisticuffs were so rare as to be practically non-existent.

Because of the essentially transitory nature of our rela-tionships — people were coming and going all the time as the time-served left and replacements arrived — close friendships were not common. First names were seldom used — we were generally addressed by a nickname of some sort. Often this would be an abbreviation or corruption of a surname, or a reference to a physical peculiarity. All Scotsmen were Jock, "Midlanders" were Brum, and so on, with the addition of the surname where necessary for identification.

My own nickname was Hank, from a perceived similarity between my surname and that of the prolific American pulp fiction writer Hank Janson, whose lurid novels were coveted and eagerly devoured by all and sundry. Whenever a new arrival proved to have the latest edition in his possession, he would be assailed by a chorus of "Twos up!" This curious expression was recognised throughout the Army as the means of reserving one's position of next in line. It was taken very seriously, and any attempt to jump the queue was vigorously resisted.

Books of any kind were scarce and hard to come by, and they ended up dog- eared and tattered as they did the rounds of the camp. Off-duty hours were spent playing cards (which I didn't much care for, and seldom engaged in), reading, writing letters, or just gossiping, and probably smoking more cigarettes than were good for us.

There was not a great deal of social interaction between the occupants of different tents — generally our leisure time was spent indoors, there being little opportunity for outdoor activities. The inmates of the tent next to ours were nearly all Scotsmen, and in a demonstration of national pride they had put up a sign at the entrance of their residence reading "OOR AIN WEE HOOSE", in a refreshing touch of frivolity that would never have been tolerated in a home posting! They had managed to get a dartboard from somewhere, and so we were able to have a game now and then, which made a nice change.

In the third tent on our side of the camp there were a mob

of New Zealanders, members of the Royal NZ Corps of Signals. Among them was a Maori named Pablo, or so he called himself. He was a very nice, friendly sort of bloke when he was sober, but when he had had a couple of beers he became very belligerent, proclaiming his intention to murder any "Pommie Bastards" that got in his way. Nobody took any notice of him when he was in this state, because he was in such a near-legless condition that he didn't really pose much of a threat!

On the train from Cornwall to London after my embarkation leave I had fallen into conversation with a group of schoolgirls from Newquay Grammar School; they were 6m formers, seventeen or eighteen years old, and were on their way to France on an exchange visit with French girls of the same age group. This was part of a government-sponsored scheme, in which a group of English students would travel to France, where they would spend a couple of weeks, each staying with a French family and attending school with their host's children. At the end of their stay would return to Britain, accompanied by their new-found friends. The scheme also applied to boys in the same manner, co-ed schools being rare in those days.

Naturally the girls were in a festive mood, and were cheerful company on the long rail journey. I was particularly attracted to one of them, a pretty, vivacious blonde girl named Pearl. In London of course we went our separate ways, and I thought no more of the incident than as of a very pleasant interlude.

Now, in Korea, far from home and lonely, and not having a girl to write to, my thoughts turned to Pearl. I decided that I would write to her and see what happened what have I got to lose, I thought.

I didn't know her address of course, nor even her surname. Undeterred, I composed a nice friendly letter, addressed it to

"Miss Pearl _____, 6th Form, Newquay Grammar School, Cornwall, England, and sent it off, without any great hope of success. Rather to my surprise, and certainly my delight, a week or so later I received a reply in much the same vein as mine had been. Pearl wrote that when my letter arrived she had been hauled into the Headmistress's office to "please explain!"

For the rest of the time I spent in Korea, Pearl and I kept up a sort of pen friendship, on a more or less regular, if infrequent basis. She even sent me a photograph, which I proudly displayed on top of the packing crate that served as my locker. When I returned to Britain, I visited her and her family a few times at their home in Newquay, and we went out together for a while. However, our relationship never developed into anything more serious, and in the manner of such things, we eventually drifted apart. But I was very grateful to her for having made my Army service so much more pleasant than it otherwise would have been.

My position in C.B. Troop as chief GD wallah had many advantages — unless there was a particular job somebody in authority wanted done, I was left very much alone to take care of the routine maintenance of the place. Even when there was something special to do, the N.C.O. concerned would just explain to me what was required, and leave me to it. Normally I had the two Kims as my crew, with the addition of one or two others for the bigger jobs, and for most of the time I was my own boss.

Suddenly though everything changed. One of the batmen, his time expired, left us, and I was appointed to take his place. To me this had all the hallmarks of a minor disaster. I knew immediately that there had been a dreadful mistake. My mental image of the ideal batman was of a person who could instinctively anticipate his master's every wish, and who would willingly, cheerfully, and deferentially conform to those wishes. I was not that person. Like most people, I have always been ready to lend anyone a hand where there is a need for it. However, I have a deep seated aversion to doing for people things that they are quite capable of doing for themselves. As far as I could see, cleaning another man's boots, no matter who he is, or looking after his kit, or making his bed, or organising the collection and return of his laundry, or tidying up his tent, or, perhaps worst of all, fetching him an early morning cup of tea from the Officers' Mess — none of these things is likely to make a meaningful contribution to the war effort. Where there is an element of compulsion, the situation quickly becomes intolerable.

Since we were on active service, and therefore chronically short of manpower, I was allocated three officers to look after, a captain and two 2nd lieutenants. These last two were run of the mill NS junior officers, lacking in confidence and generally fairly ineffectual, but the captain was a very good officer indeed. He enjoyed wide popularity amongst the men, for he was one of Nature's gentlemen, courteous to all while being firm and decisive. He had come up through the ranks, and had none of the arrogance often found in the products of Sandhurst.

It was said that he had been awarded the Military Cross for gallantry — one of his actions had been to call down fire on his own position when it was in danger of being overrun. All this of course I learned from others — it was never mentioned in his presence. Anyway, he was one of the few officers that I genuinely both liked and respected.

The first chance I got, the day I began my new job, I raised with the captain my misgivings about my suitability for the position. I even mentioned to him that it was my understanding that batmen were volunteers, and that those who had an objection to the job could not be forced to take it. This was in fact a widely held belief, based probably on yet another false rumour started long ago by one of the many "barrack room lawyers" that infest the Army. The captain gently disabused me of the notion — he produced a copy of the "Queen's Rules and Regulations", and turned to the section that dealt with the legality and otherwise of orders. There it was, in black and white, given as an example of a "Legitimate Order", the irrefutable phrase "To act as Batman."

Thus it seemed that my fate was sealed. Unbeknown to me, however, salvation was at hand. The captain, moved by pity, or perhaps more by the realisation that my sullen acceptance, and patent lack of enthusiasm boded ill for the success of the enforced arrangement, had me relieved of the position, and an alternative found.

It had probably not been too difficult to replace me, because the batman's job was seen by many blokes as a cushy number — the tasks involved were not onerous; it was a bit of a skive in many ways. The biggest disadvantage was the need to be up with the lark for the morning tea routine. Once the officers were about their daily business, the batman was left alone to do what was required, with no interference from anyone. It was just that I didn't like the job, and was mightily relieved that my career as a khaki-clad Jeeves had lasted a mere three days. Happy to be back with the Kims, I carried on as before, until a couple of weeks later fate once again intervened.

10

THE COMMAND POST

This time the reason was that a vacancy had arisen in the Command Post staff, due again of course to the incumbent having served his time. For whatever reason I was elected to fill the void. Perhaps the powers that be thought that my earlier training as a radar operator was somehow relevant, and indeed that had probably been the rationale for posting me to C.B. Troop in the first place. In any case I was delighted with the development — after all the Command Post was the nerve centre of C.B. Tp. the very reason for our existence.

The CP staff consisted of sundry officers, a few N.C.O.s, and a number of Gunners, who were either Signallers, who operated the radio-sets, or Counter Bombardment Officer's assistants known as CBO-Acks., of whom I was to be one. I was vaguely familiar with the layout of the CP bunker, but now that I was part of the crew, I soon became intimately involved with the running of the place.

Basically the job of the CBO-Ack was to receive reports of enemy activity from our observation posts (OPS), and to correlate the information so that the appropriate response could be calculated. Most of the data we got was in the form of reports of shelling, called "Shelreps." These generally came in by phone, but often by radio if the lines were down.

Interestingly, the control knobs on the radio sets we had

were labelled in Russian. I gathered that these sets had originally been destined for shipment to the U.S.S.R. on the so-called "Murmansk Run", as part of Britain's war aid to the Red Army, but had somehow been "diverted"!

We had blank shelrep forms, marked in lines "A" to "I", which we filled in with the information received from the OPS. "A" was for the Brigade No. (The three brigades were numbered 12, 32, and 52). Each brigade had several OPS, and these all had numbers ending in 5 — 15, 25, 35 and so on. These were identified in line "B". "C" gave the compass bearing of the gun flash from the OP," "D" was the time the shelling began, and "E" the time it ended. "F" was the area being shelled, "G" the number and type of the enemy guns involved, "H" the perceived purpose of the shelling i.e. registration, harassing etc., and "I" the number of rounds fired.

Telephone and radio procedures were very strict, and rigidly observed. Messages were relayed in accordance with a prescribed formula — idle chit-chat was forbidden. One of the sacred cows in this respect was the word "repeat" — if you missed part of a message, or did not understand it, you said "Say again, over." Never, never were you to say "Repeat, over." The only time "repeat" was used in the Artillery was as an order to a gun crew to loose off the same number of rounds at the same range and bearing as in the previous salvo. One can imagine the mayhem that might ensue if such an order were given by mistake!

There was often a good deal of atmospheric interference in the radio transmissions, which did at times cause some difficulties. The OP operators were all very experienced signallers, and rattled off the shelreps at an alarming rate, so that in the beginning I had trouble keeping up, and had to employ a sort of improvised shorthand to scribble down the data on a scrap of paper and fill in the shelrep forms properly when things settled down a bit. The OP blokes could become a trifle sarcastic if they heard "Say again" too often! But after a while I got the hang of it, and managed as well as any of the others.

The OP signaller would initiate a shelrep by calling his brigade number e.g. 32, and announcing: "32 shelrep, over", to which our reply was: "32, go ahead, over." The ensuing report would go something like this:-

"Three two shelrep,
Baker: Three five
Charlie: Two nine five degrees
Dog: Oh nine fifty hours
Easy: Oh nine fifty two hours
Fox: Friends on left
George: One by one-oh-five mike mike (i.e. one 105 mm. Gun)
How: Registration
Item: Four rounds
Roger? Over.

To which our reply would be: "Roger, Out.", "Roger" being the code for "Message received and understood."

If there were more than one shelrep to be sent, the OP would ask after each one "Roger so far? Over", to which our reply would be "Roger, over, and so it would go on. By thus sticking to routine, everybody knew what was going on, and there were no misunderstandings.

On our chart table was a map of the division's sector, on which we plotted the data from the shelreps. At this late stage of the proceedings the war had become a fairly static affair — there was no longer hope on either side of an outright victory. Rather, both sides were prepared to settle for an honourable draw! The only sticking point was to reach agreement on the precise terms of a ceasefire. Consensus was tantalisingly close on several occasions, only to see the negotiations collapse once again. In fact, despite the increasing futility of continuing the struggle, there were many fiercely fought battles in these latter days, as both sides strove to hold their territory, or even to seize a bit more of the enemy's, in order to improve their bargaining power.

Because of the more or less fixed positions of the battle lines, we knew where the enemy guns were — they were all marked on our map, together with the locations of our OPs. Only rarely was a new enemy gun position identified, and this would be plotted when we received the information from the OPs, in the form of a "Location Report" or Locrep, which was rather more complicated than a shelrep.

From the details supplied by the shelrep, we would draw a line from the OP's on the given bearing, and any hostile gun on or near the line was suspected of being the trouble-maker. When the same gun flash was reported by two OPs, which was often the case, we could be pretty sure that a gun lying on or close to the intersection of the two lines was the guilty party. On rare occasions we even got three sightings, and in those cases the intersection of the lines formed a small triangle, due to slight inaccuracies in the bearings we were given.

When an enemy gun position was confirmed as being a nuisance, it received some attention from our gunners, and soon ceased to be a problem. However, the relief was quite often only temporary, because the Chinese had a trick of digging a tunnel into the side of a hill — they had a seemingly inexhaustible supply of labour - and then mounting a gun on rails inside the tunnel.

They were then able to trundle the gun up to the mouth of the tunnel, fire off a few rounds, and drag it back to safety before we could respond. The only way to deal with that situation was to block the tunnel with a few well-directed rounds, and enjoy some respite while they dug it out again.

The workload in the CP varied greatly from day to day, depending of course on the level of activity at the front. Sometimes it was a veritable madhouse, with reports coming in thick and fast, so that the phones ran hot and the radios were in constant use. At other times everything was deathly still, often for hours at a time. As I mentioned before, the CP was manned at all times, busy or not. We worked in twelve hour shifts, changing at 0800hrs and 2000hrs. During the day shift there were two CBO-Acks and a couple of signallers present, and an officer or two. At night we managed with one of each, except when the Chinese decided to launch an attack (often at the time of a full moon), and then we might have to call for reinforcements.

On very quiet nights when there was little or no activity at the front, it was our custom for the signaler and the CBOA to take turns having a bit of a nap. One hot, humid night when I was "on watch" I nodded off and missed a call from an OP asking for a "report of signals" (to check his radio was "on net"). One of the officers, a major, had an extension of our radio in his tent and noted that the OP was not receiving any reply, so he came to the CP to investigate. The result was that the signaler and I were put on a charge. The case was heard by another major, who stated that he was aware of the practice of napping and asked which of us had been "on duty" at the time. When I confessed to my guilt he freed my co-accused and fined me four week's pay and that was that.

Looking back, our system was very primitive in comparison

to the technological advances that have been made in warfare these days, but we managed quite well on the whole, since we were confronted with an enemy whose methods were even less sophisticated than our own. There was a story about the earlier days of the war, when there was more mobility in the fighting than there was now. It seems that a U .S. Army command truck containing teletype equipment and much important and sensitive data had been captured by the Chinese. This event naturally caused a fair amount of consternation at the time, but when the tide of battle later turned and the truck was recaptured, it was discovered that the fears were unfounded. The Chinese, unable to make head or tail of the contents, had thrown it all out, and had used the truck as a mobile toilet for their officers.

I suppose there is one in every group; what is known in Army parlance as a "Manky Bastard" — that is one who is incorrigibly and systematically dirty, scruffy and untidy. Ours was a "Lancashire man" who occupied one of the corner bunks in the tent. Nobody could remember ever having seen him have a shower or even a good wash. How he had managed to survive basic training was a matter of conjecture! He was always the last to go to bed, and first up in the morning, so it was not clear whether or not he undressed at night. I remember one particular night, when there was an unusually high level of activity in the forward areas, (the Duke of Wellington's especially were involved in heavy fighting), and our MB lay on his bunk all night fully dressed, boots and all, so as to be ready for the off in case our lines broke, compelling us to "bug out", to use that dreadful American expression. The rest of us, having more faith in our front-line comrades, went to bed as usual. As expected, The Comwel Div's line held firm.

The least attractive aspect of the MB's conduct were the shameless letters he wrote to his girlfriend, which he often insisted on reading aloud to anyone silly enough to listen. He would describe in gory detail non-existent battles in which he claimed to have played a central role. The despicable practice was universally condemned.

He did however fulfil one useful purpose. It was the rule that the last one to bed would switch off the Tilley lamp, our sole form of lighting in the tent. This involved releasing the pressure valve, so that the light went out by itself. In the warm and humid evenings there would be swarms of mosquitoes around the lamp, and when the light went out they would make a beeline for the nearest available heat source. If you weren't quick and lively getting under your mozzie net, one or two of the blighters would get in with you. In a confined space a mozzie makes a horrible, high- pitched whining sound, and when the whining stops you know one of them has landed on you. You can then expect a sharp nip, resulting in an itchy lump. Due to his nocturnal habits, the MB was generally the victim!

Of course there was little danger that mozzie bites would cause anything but minor irritation — the daily Paludrine tablets I mentioned earlier saw to that. In fact there was very little sickness of any kind among us. We were young and in good health to begin with, otherwise we wouldn't have been there in the first place, and the worst we had to put up with were tinea or so-called athlete's foot, and prickly heat, brought about by the heat and humidity. To combat these irritations we were issued with tins of powder, which proved to be very effective. Furthermore our diet, though uninspiring, was nutritious enough to keep our immune systems active.

There did exist in Korea at the time a virulent disease which, if not treated promptly, could be fatal. This was haemorrhagic fever, known locally as songo. It was said to cause many unpleasant symptoms, including bleeding from the pores. We were mercifully spared any experience of this scourge, which apparently was caused by exposure to parasites carried by rats. In our camp there was never any sign of rodents, or any other wildlife either for that matter, except of course for flies and the ubiquitous mosquitoes.

One evening the humdrum existence of the camp was interrupted by an alarming incident. All was quiet, as there was a temporary lull in activity at the front. I was sitting on my bunk, writing one of my infrequent letters home. There were a few other blokes in the tent at the time, similarly occupied or just relaxing or perhaps reading. One of these was our bombardier, who had the bunk opposite mine. He was a decent sort of bloke for a regular, not inflated with self-importance like some of them.

Anyway, our peace was suddenly shattered by a burst of machine gun fire. My pen flew one way, my writing pad the other, and I hit the deck all in one fluent movement — poetry in motion it must have been! Without thought I grabbed my rifle and levered a round into the breech. All the others reacted in a similar fashion, and one after another, led by the bombardier, we slithered out under the tent flap and into the monsoon ditch which ran the length of the tent outside. The primary purpose of the trenches was to prevent the flooding of the tents during the heavy monsoonal downpours, and were not really deep enough to afford much protection in the present circumstances, though they were better than nothing. There was no more firing, but we remained huddled there for a minute or two, until word came that the scare was over.

What had happened was that the Troop Bren gunner, a bloke named Tom, had suddenly gone "troppo", and emptied a magazine of ammunition through the tent roof. When the magazine was empty his tent-mates had grabbed him and disarmed him before he could reload. Tom had been in Korea for over a year, and was due for repatriation in a couple of months, but had for some reason cracked. He was placed on a charge and marched directly to the guard room, the case to be heard the next morning.

The Army has its own legal system, based on the premise that an overly strict observance of civil rights has a deleterious effect on discipline. As far as I could make out it has three ways of administering justice. For minor misdemeanours officers, as well as in some cases N .C.O.s, have the right to impose penalties without reference to higher authority. Punishments are generally quite lenient, extra fatigues perhaps, or doubling around the square a few times with rifle held above the head — things like that. In home postings a favourite was of course the traditional "Confined to Barracks", but in our situation this was recognised as a futile exercise. Our isolation from the world at large meant that we had nowhere to go anyway, and no means of getting there!

Where there was a more serious offence, like insubordination, abusing a superior, stealing Government property, or going AWOL, the miscreant would be placed on a formal charge. In the Artillery a charge was familiarly known as a "fizzer", an allusion to the fuse on a shell, which when activated had a similar capacity to cause somebody considerable grief!

Charges are heard by the C.O., or if he is not available, by the next senior officer. The ruling is absolute — there is no appeal. The prisoner may speak on his own behalf, but argument is nearly always a waste of time, and may even irritate the judge into passing a stiffer sentence!

Before entering the orderly room, where the C.O. is already seated behind a desk, the accused is ordered to remove his hat and belt. This little ceremony is a traditional one, whose origin lies in the dim and distant past, when a disgruntled prisoner, outraged at the sentence pronounced upon him, had assaulted the presiding officer with his shako. Thus deprived of any potential weapon, the prisoner is escorted at the double into the room, ordered to mark time, turn to face the officer, and then halt. The officer, having been informed of the nature of the offence, questions the accused, hears any witnesses to the incident, and then makes his judgement and passes sentence, after which the condemned man is marched out, again at the double.

Really grave crimes, such as murder, desertion, cowardice in the face of the enemy, a vicious attack on a Superior and so on, are referred to a court-martial. A court-martial is a very serious business indeed, and is not convened lightly. The case is heard by a panel of senior officers, and there are prosecution and defence counsel in attendance. Where there is a conviction, a lengthy jail sentence is the usual result, and even a dishonourable discharge in extreme Cases. In earlier times floggings, or perhaps the death penalty might have been imposed, but there has been some progress!

In the event, for his misdemeanour, Tom was ordered to serve twenty eight days in the detention centre, which was located near Pusan. That was a severe enough punishment, for the centre had a fearsome reputation. It was staffed largely by French-Canadians, many of whom were by nature hostile to anyone whose native tongue was English. This tendency may have had something to do with resentment about General Wolfe's victory over Montcalm on the Heights of Abraham, a skirmish that gave Britain control of the fledgling colony, though it cost Wolfe his life.

It may also be that the motto on the Vandoos' cap badge — "JE ME SOUVIENS" I REMEMBER refers to the same event. Whatever the cause, the animosity was there.

Sometime previously one of our cooks, a Catering Corps bloke, had been caught selling chocolate and other good things to the Korean civilians, and for his sins had received four weeks' detention. He was cocky, cheeky sort of chap when he went to Pusan, but when he returned he was a changed man — quiet, withdrawn, and ready to jump at his own shadow.

It so happened that one night, a week or two before his escapade with the Bren gun, Tom and an accomplice had managed to gain access to a Jeep, and had driven to a village far to the south in search of romance and whatever else they could find. The result was that they returned with a small pig which they had somehow acquired from some luckless farmer. The animal was settled into the trench behind Tom's tent, and Tom reckoned that he would feed it on scraps from the cookhouse for a few weeks.

Then he would butcher it to provide pork chops for a barbecue at his farewell do. Unfortunately Fate intervened to spoil his little plan. While he was away in the slammer, a recent arrival at C.B. Troop chanced to be on guard duty. This fellow had heard that there were a lot of wild pigs roaming around the hills and vales of Korea, and that these creatures were extremely dangerous and aggressive. So while he was taking his turn as prowler, and heard Tom's pig grunting, he naturally thought that here was a wild boar that had accidentally fallen into the trench, whereupon he promptly shot the wretched beast.

There was great consternation when the facts of the mishap became known, for everyone was aware that at best Tom was of an unpredictable nature and there was no telling what he might do when he returned and learned of his loss. Although he had been compelled to surrender stewardship Of the Bren, he was capable of doing much damage with his bare hands. After some discussion it was decided that Tom would be told that the pig had by some means contrived to escape from the trench, and had vanished without trace. To lend credence to the story, marks were scratched in the end wall of the trench to simulate the escape route. The ruse worked, and though he was greatly disappointed at the turn of events, Tom was consoled by the thought of his impending departure for home. And so the episode came to an end without further damage, and life resumed its humdrum routine.

Not far from our camp there was a large compound housing a battalion of U .S. Army engineers. They were very security conscious, and their encampment was surrounded by a high fence topped with barbed wire. At intervals along the fence there were ominous and rather forbidding notices, which read:

"COME IN THROUGH THE GATE
AND VISIT YOUR FRIENDS -
COME IN OVER THE FENCE
AND VISIT YOUR ANCESTORS!"

They were not nearly as inhospitable as the warning suggested though, and we became quite chummy with some of them. Occasionally a few of us would be invited over there to enjoy a film show, a real treat for us as we had very little entertainment of our own. That was one of the few disadvantages of being a small unit — because of our small number we never had visits from concert parties or the like, and had to rely on the generosity of larger units.

On one occasion a couple of us were invited to join in a baseball game with the engineers. I had never had anything to do with the game before, and found it was very different from the more familiar cricket. For one thing there was a great deal of what we nowadays we call "sledging." At the time it seemed most unsportsmanlike to me — it was virtually unknown in cricket then, though it has unfortunately become accepted practice in modern times. The Americans had already developed the tactic of verbal abuse into an art form, and nobody seemed to take any offence at it.

Not only were the engineers handy neighbours in the field of entertainment, but were also useful trading partners. One of them in particular, with whom I became friendly, developed a great fondness for Cadbury's milk chocolate, which we were able to buy cheaply from the NAAFI truck on its more or less fortnightly visits, but which was unobtainable by the Americans from their PX canteens. For a ½ lb. bar of the delicacy, my friend would readily give a carton of 200 Lucky Strike or Chesterfield cigarettes, a very favourable rate of exchange!

From the same bloke I once got an American bayonet for a spare one of ours that I happened to have. The bayonets with which the Artillery was issued were of simple design — no handle, just a spike with a bracket that clipped on the end of a rifle. It was not anticipated that the Gunners would have much cause to use a bayonet, except perhaps to pierce holes in a can of tinned milk! Our infantry had bayonets of a similar type, but with a proper blade instead of a spike. The "pig sticker," as it was called, fascinated the Americans, whose own bayonets were of the traditional type, like a small sword.

Another acquisition from that period, which I still have, was one of those remarkable cigarette lighters, the legendary "Zippo." These iconic treasures were sold to GIs through the PX for a dollar a piece, and were worth much more. They were beautifully simple in design, so durable that they carried an unconditional lifetime guarantee. If your Zippo failed for any reason, all you had to do was to send it to the manufacturers in Bradford, Pennsylvania, and you would receive a new one free of charge.

The lighter consisted of a stainless steel outer casing with a flip up lid, and an inner section containing the working parts. The inner casing held cotton wool padding, flint and flint wheel, and a virtually indestructible fibreglass wick protected by a wind guard so effective that the lighter was practically storm proof. In those days before the advent of propane gas, lighters used as fuel a form of high octane gasoline known as lighter fluid, but since in our situation this was not readily available, the usual method of refueling was to remove the inner casing, hook a piece of wire through the wind guard, and immerse it in the fuel tank of the nearest Jeep for a few seconds until the cotton wool was well saturated. Then the excess was shaken off and the lighter reassembled. It was then good for another month or two.

Zippos are still on the market today, indistinguishable from the original, and still carry the lifetime guarantee, proof indeed of the futility of trying to improve on perfection!

There was another American unit, a much smaller one this time, consisting of half a dozen GIs, members of the U.S.Army Signal Corps. They formed the Air- Ground Liaison team, and as the name suggests, their job was to maintain contact between the ground forces and the U. S. Air Force squadrons so as to co-ordinate joint operations between the two. Their work was very hush-hush, and was conducted in a command truck of the same type as the one which the Chinese had once captured, used, abused, and abandoned, as described earlier. This little group was self-contained and were all privates or NCOs — not an officer in sight. As an added luxury they had a Korean houseboy to do their cooking and menial chores.

One of these fellows, a Californian named Wayne Messick,

became a close friend of mine. He was a talented guitar player and a good singer, being especially fond of Country and Western music, of which he had a vast repertoire. I was very sorry to see him go, when a few months after the truce was signed, he was transferred to a Special Services unit which provided concert parties to entertain troops all over the country. But we kept in touch with each other, and got together for a few beers whenever we got the chance. We even exchanged letters for several years after we had returned to our homes.

11

CEASE FIRE

I had been working in the Command Post for several weeks, and felt that I was now a competent operator, when another life-changing event took place. With a suddenness that took almost everybody by surprise, after the many false starts over the past two years, at 1000hrs on the 27th of July 1953, the U.N. and the Chinese chief negotiators finally put pen to paper, and the cease-fire agreement was signed, with the guns to fall silent twelve hours later. Presumably the delay was to allow time for the glad tidings to reach the furthest corners of the war zone.

When the good news finally sank in that the war was actually over, there was almost universal rejoicing. The only ones to have been less than pleased would have been Syngman Rhee and his henchmen, who had long cherished the hope that there would be a different outcome, one which would have seen them ruling a united Korea. In fact Rhee did not himself sign the agreement, and there was never a formal treaty, only a truce. This is only one of many factors which have complicated the stability of the ceasefire agreement over the years, preventing a permanent peace solution between North and South Korea.

Nevertheless the rest of us were, to use a well-worn Army expression largely unintelligible to the average civilian, "chuffed to little NAAFI breaks" — that is to say extremely pleased, that the madness was over. The folly of it all was that after all the killing and wounding, the disruption of homeless families and the widespread devastation, the situation was very much as it had been before the outbreak of war — the country was still divided more or less at the 38th parallel, and the main difference was that now there were more widows and orphans than there had been in 1950.

So for us it was a time of wild celebration. Large quantities of bottled Asahi beer were consumed with great gusto, resulting in many sore heads and empty pockets. There was also much singing, with huge enthusiasm and rather less harmony!

Every war gives rise to its own peculiar songs — for example, the rollicking "Pack up your troubles in your old kit bag", or the encouraging "Keep the home fires burning" are forever associated with the First World War, while memories of the Second are evoked by the wistful "Lili Marlene", or Vera Lynn's classic "White Cliffs of Dover." The Korean War also spawned a few of its own.

Probably our favourite was one borrowed from the Americans, a satirical parody of Country singer Hank Snow's "I'm movin' on."

Our version began like this:

"When you hear the pitter-patter of a thousand feet,
it's the Commonwealth Division in full retreat —
we're movin' on, we'll soon be gone.
They're getting' too far down the MSR
so we're movin' on."

Other verses in like vein followed — here are a few of them: -

"Ashes to ashes and dust to dust,
If the Gooks don't get us, then the Chinkies must,
we're movin' on, we'll soon be gone.

When you get to Pusan, don't cause a jam,
Keep movin' on."
"The Chinks are comin' over Three-Five-Five,*
The Durhams are doin' the Shuckland Jive,
They're movin' on ....."

"There's Mamasan goin' down the track,
With a GI baby on her back,
she's movin' on....."

"The Chinks came over the mountain pass,
Playin' the Burp Gun Boogie on the RCR's ass,
They're movin' on ...."

And so it went on. There were one or two of the blokes who were very good at making up more verses, of which some survived and others were discarded. The appeal of this song was that verses could be added, altered or omitted to suit the circumstances, and poke fun at whoever happened to be in the news at the time.

I was reminded of this many years later by that excellent BBC TV show hosted by David Frost, "That Was The Week That Was", in which Lance Percival very cleverly made up impromptu Calypso songs on whatever subject he was given.

---

* (Three-Five-Five: - a hill in our sector, so called from its height in metres above sea level. There was also a hill 187, and another known as the Hook from the shape of its crest. All had been at one time or another the scene of fierce fighting).

Another popular one, especially with the British, was entitled "Sygman Rhee." It went like this, -

"I was back in Blighty, having lots of fun,
when the war broke out in Korea and they handed me a gun.
They said "You're going to Korea to make the Commies run,
and to fight for the bastard Syngman Rhee."

Chorus:
"Syngman Rhee, Syngman Rhee,
Fighting for the bastard Syngman Rhee."

"We landed there in Pusan and it wasn't very nice —
we didn't come to Korea to eat their bloody rice,
But to fight for the bastard Syngman Rhee."

Chorus:
"Well, the blood it was running, and I was running too;
around the hills of Korea, with nothing else to do
But to fight for the bastard Syngman Rhee."

Chorus:
"Why are you running — are you afraid to die?"
"The reason that I'm running is because I cannot fly,
and I'm fighting for the bastard Syngman Rhee."

Chorus....
"When I get back to Blighty I'll be having lots of fun,
and I'll never turn my face again towards the Rising Sun,
Just to fight for the bastard Syngman Rhee."
Chorus...

The Canadians had a song of their Own, to the tune of "The Mountains of Mourne," which told the Story of a poor RCR soldier who was deprived of his week's leave in Tokyo by the Provost (Canadian equivalent of our Military Police), for having "mud on your tunic and blood on your sleeve", and who roundly abuses "the Army's Disgrace" for being so officious.

There were of course several other songs to add variety to these boozy sessions, many of them being, in the nature of things, quite bawdy and unfit to be performed in mixed company!

After a few nights of this kind of revelry, the reality of our new situation began to sink in, and paradoxically — perversely even, a feeling of emptiness overtook many of us. Suddenly and unexpectedly our raison d 'etre had disappeared, and we felt that we were in limbo. As one would expect, rumours and speculation were rife — what would happen to us now, would we be transferred to another theatre somewhere, Malaya perhaps? Maybe instead of bringing troops out from Britain as replacements for those whose time was up, we would be sent there, or to somewhere else where things were not too healthy. It was too much to hope that our next destination would be a cushy number like Hong Kong!

By far the most horrendous suggestion was that the U. N. might decide to send troops to the aid of the beleaguered French in Indo-China, where they were having great difficulty in suppressing the local insurgents. If that were to happen, we would be in the prime position for selection!

I am pleased to say that nothing came of that speculation: I would hate to have had any involvement in the fiasco that followed the final defeat of the French forces by the Viet Mihn at Dien Bien Phu in 1954.

As it turned out, after the rumour mill had had a good run,

it became clear that we were not going anywhere. Despite the goodwill shown (at last!) at the conference table, there was still a deep-seated mistrust between the two sides. It was feared that even a minor incident at the border might be misconstrued, and set the whole thing off again. The best we could hope for was that the ceasefire would hold, and that further talks would continue until some sort of permanent agreement could be reached.

In spite of Rhee's chagrin, both the U.N. and the Chinese were reasonably satisfied with the present position — the U.N. felt that they had achieved the purpose of their mission, which had started out as a "police action" to oust the Communist forces from South Korea, while the Chinese were content with having gained face by holding the might of the American military machine to a draw after Macarthur's threat to invade Manchuria, if not the Chinese homeland.

So both sides withdrew their front line troops to a sufficient distance from each other to create a "De-Militarised Zone"or DMZ, thus minimising the risk of any accidental flare-ups. The UN authorities had already made plans for such a move, and had partially prepared defensive positions along what was known as the "Kansas Line"

Although CB Troop had been allocated a position in the proposed defensive line, to which we would retire if hostilities were resumed, it was not considered necessary for us to move while the truce held, so we stayed put. Later on we did engage in some field manoeuvres in our Kansas Line positions, but these were only two or three day exercises at most, and we never did set up permanent camp there. These exercises were held every few months, just to keep us occupied, I suppose, and to remind us that we were still Soldiers of the Queen, and in a potentially hostile country!

The procedure in these schemes was to pack up all our essential gear, often at night, and head for the Kansas Line, where as a first priority guards were posted, and duty operators allocated to set up and man the command truck. The next job was to erect our tents, and try to get a bit of sleep for what was left of the night. The exercises were held in conjunction with other units, so telephone and radio contact was established with them, and practice communications simulating battle conditions were conducted. Everything was taken very seriously by our officers and senior NCOs: perhaps less so by the rank and file. Our preoccupation was to get back to the relative comfort of our normal camp, and never mind the war games!

The accommodation on manoeuvres consisted of two-man bivouac tents that you could barely crawl into, with scant room for two sleeping bags. The food served by the camp kitchen left much to be desired, while the primitive nature of the latrine and ablution facilities made those at CB Tp. seem positively luxurious. Our Kansas Line position lay in a shallow valley in which Korean farmers were now growing crops, and I remember one particular farmer who, quite justifiably I thought, was outraged by the wanton trampling of his millet crop as our vehicles were manoeuvred into their positions.

On one of these schemes, in the middle of the winter, we were subjected to a simulated strafing attack by a couple of Sabre jets. It was a truly frightening experience as the aircraft screamed up the valley at low altitude over our heads, then turned and roared back on another run in case they had missed any of us! It was not difficult to imagine the demoralising effect such sorties would have had on the Chinese infantry, especially when the planes were armed with napalm bombs.

However, in the immediate aftermath of the ceasefire there

was no time for such fun and games — those were to come later. Very soon after the signing of the truce there were more pressing matters to be addressed, as negotiations began about the vexed question of the return of prisoners of war. As we shall see, the issue gave rise to a fair bit of jockeying for advantage in the propaganda war.

12

BRITANNIA CAMP

The exchange of POWs was scheduled to begin shortly after the signing of the truce, and to be completed within 90 days, but there were some preliminary preparations to be made beforehand. It had been decided that a reception centre for Commonwealth troops would be established on the site of what had till now been a Canadian Army field hospital, and which lay several miles to the south. It was of course an obvious choice, since all the medical facilities and personnel required for the examination and treatment of the returning prisoners were already in place.

The hospital had been a semi-permanent establishment, so all the buildings were wooden huts rather than tents. The wet canteen in particular was a work of art. The outside walls were covered with flattened beer cans nailed to the timber like shingles, adding to the charm of the place. As to be expected, many pleasant evenings were spent there! On one occasion we were entertained by a piper from the Black Watch, who gave a spirited rendition of all the favourite Scottish tunes on what we Sassenachs irreverently referred to as the Pigskin Piano.

One of the plans was to transfer a number of people from CB Troop to the centre, which was to be called Britannia Camp, to do whatever was necessary in the way of preparing the living quarters for the POWs, and then to act as a kind of welcoming committee for the returnees. Only about half of the Troop would be needed for the purpose — the rest would stay behind and hold the fort, as it were.

I was one of those privileged ones that went, and I was subsequently very glad to have been included, for it turned out to be a rewarding experience. We were very comfortably housed in one of the huts, and found that the food was a good deal better than we were used to, so we settled in quite readily.

The BSM in charge of our little group conceived the notion that it would be good for our morale if we had a sign outside our hut identifying us as members of the Royal Artillery, no less in fact than CB Troop. For the purpose the sign would be painted in our regimental colours, red and blue, with white lettering. Full of enthusiasm, he set about requisitioning the necessary materials, and had soon scared up some tins of paint and a few brushes. He struck one problem though — there was no blue paint to be found in the near vicinity. The only colours he could find were red, white, green, and yellow. Undeterred by the setback, he declared that he would soon rectify the situation — we would mix the green and yellow paint together, thus creating blue. It was well known, he said, that mixing blue and yellow resulted in green. On the same principle, he reasoned, his plan would achieve a similarly favourable outcome. When I rather diffidently pointed out (for he was notoriously irascible) that using that theory, mixing blue and green ought to result in yellow, but that that was very unlikely, he thought about it for a while, finally conceding that perhaps I was right. In a foul temper he strode off to continue his search further afield. His persistence ultimately paid off, and he triumphantly returned with a tin of blue paint which he had managed to beg, borrow, or steal from somewhere. I was glad for his sake, for he obviously set great store by his pet project.

However, I could not help reflecting that it was the kind of obtuseness that he had shown that had led many observers to conclude that the words "military" and "intelligence" ought never to appear in the same sentence!

The camp was ready well in time to receive the first of our guests when they started to arrive by truck from the hand-over point at Pan Mun Jom in the DMZ where the truce had been signed. I was told by one of the later arrivals that the first ones to be released had been those whom the Chinese referred to as "progressives", meaning those who had been more receptive of the "education" (what we would describe as "brain washing"), to which the prisoners, seated uncomfortably on wooden benches, were subjected in seemingly endless "lectures." These sessions consisted in the main of political rantings about the evils of Capitalism and the joys of life in the People's Republic, and were treated by the prisoners with a mixture of boredom and mild derision. The Chinese had hoped to persuade large numbers of prisoners to defect, and refuse repatriation to their former bondage, choosing instead to settle in the "Workers' Paradise." In this way they would have achieved tremendous propaganda advantage. They were, however, sadly disappointed in their efforts — from what I could gather only two British and twenty-odd Americans prisoners decided not to return home. It had been hoped that black Americans in particular would respond favourably to the brainwashing, glad of the chance to escape from their downtrodden existence in the U.S.A. In fact there was not one black prisoner among the American defectors.

One of the nurses, an Australian woman who had witnessed the physical condition of the POWs released from Changi prison in 1945, said she was struck by the contrast between that and the state of the men now being freed by the Chinese. Certainly the first arrivals seemed to be in reasonable health, at least physically. Some of those who came later showed more signs of mistreatment — they were what the Chinese termed "reactionaries", i.e. those who had been "recalcitrant" and resistant to education. They had been more roughly handled, and were rather less inclined to talk about their experiences. There was also some resentment towards the "progressives" who had preceded them into freedom.

One of the last to be released was Lt. Col. Carne, C.O. of the Gloucesters, who by all accounts had been particularly uncooperative, and as a result had spent a great deal of time in solitary confinement. He was greatly respected by all. There were of course quite a few other Gloucesters among the returning POWs, and one of them was a Cornishman whom I knew as Len. During the short time he was at Britannia Camp, he and I became quite friendly, and enjoyed some very convivial evenings over a beer or two in the wet canteen. In the course of our conversations I learned a lot about the conditions that he and his comrades had endured in the preceding two and a half years. He was matter-of-fact in his description of events in the POW camp, and there was little trace of bitterness in his account. I was sorry when it came time for Len to leave, but before he went he gave me as a souvenir a Christmas card which, along with other prisoners, he had received as a gesture of goodwill from the Chinese the previous Christmas. I have it still.

As well as the CB Troop contingent, there were representatives of other units then serving in Korea, who were now on the temporary staff at the camp — the Black Watch piper was one of these. Most of those people were from the infantry battalions, and among them was a French-Canadian by the name of Marcel Frechette. He was from Quebec, and was a member of the Van

Doos. Aha! I thought, here was a chance to try out my schoolboy French which was by now becoming a bit rusty from lack of use. Marcel was something of a loner, but seemed happy to have someone to talk to in his native tongue, even one as inept as I was!

He himself spoke passable English — most of the French-Canadians I met were bi-lingual to a greater or lesser extent- so we were able to carry on a reasonably coherent conversation, though I was intrigued to discover how much Canadian French had been influenced — corrupted, some would say — by the adoption of English words. For example, the Quebeckers spoke of "les patates" instead of "les pommes-de-terre" with which I was more familiar. They also used some older words that had fallen into disuse in France. I suppose there is a parallel here with the North American use of the word "fall" which had once been used in England, but had long ago been replaced by the word "autumn".

At all events Marcel was one of the many interesting people I met at Britannia Camp, and when it was time for us to return to CB Troop I could not deny a feeling of reluctance at the prospect. But go we must — our job here was finished and all the former POWs were now well on their way home to Blighty. And so ended what had undoubtedly been the most pleasant and enjoyable period of my career as a National Serviceman so far.

13

THE APPROACH OF WINTER

On arrival back at CB Troop we discovered that the rear party had not been idle in our absence. The weather-beaten tents we had left behind had disappeared, and had been replaced by brand-new ones. The new tents had side panels of white canvas, which admitted far more light than had been the case with the old ones. Moreover, our old improvised, ramshackle bunks had also been consigned to the rubbish tip, and in their places were rows of steel-frame beds complete with mattresses — thin ones to be sure, but mattresses nevertheless. All this largesse was interpreted as an indication that we would be remaining in our present location for the duration.

There was a rumour as well that our mess tent was scheduled for removal in the near future, and replacement by a Quonset hut. Unlike the majority of Army rumours, this one turned out to be true, and before long work had begun on the new structure. At this rate the CB Troop encampment would soon resemble a well- organised military establishment!

I was disappointed that there had been no attempt to upgrade our ablution facilities. Our primitive latrine and shower arrangements remained unchanged, but I realised that the lack of running water, and indeed plumbing of any kind in the camp, would have been a severe handicap in that regard.

By late autumn the new mess hall was completed and furnished with new tables and benches. It must have been a great improvement for the catering staff as well, with much bigger and better kitchen space and facilities, Wonder of wonders, we were also supplied with plates and proper cutlery — our mess tins and camping- style knife, fork and spoon sets (familiarly known as "chop sticks") could now be placed in semi-retirement against occasional use on any field manoeuvres that might be inflicted upon us. One way and another, our feeding arrangements were reminiscent of the old wartime British Restaurants.

As expected, along with all these changes there had been some change of personnel, and there were a few new faces. One of the newcomers was an eager- beaver 2nd. Lt. who hit upon the idea of identifying the CB tent by means of a number of white-washed stones on the ground outside, arranged to spell "CB TROOP — HQRA." Immediately alarm bells began to ring. If this kind of regimentation were allowed to take hold, there was no telling where it might lead! So overnight, moved by an unknown hand, the stones now spelled out a well-known vulgar expression relating to bovine excrement. In the end a compromise was reached whereby the stones were placed in a neat arc around the fire-fighting sand bucket and shovel which stood outside the tent. No further unnecessary embellishments were attempted!

It was by now late autumn, and we were getting the first taste of the impending winter. We began to receive issues of winter gear, the first of which were heavy woolen jumpers, followed soon after by white kapok-filled sleeping bags. We each got two bags which we placed one inside the other. Initially we used the bags as an extra mattress, but as winter approached and the temperature started to drop, we began to snuggle inside them in the intended manner.

Korean winters are cold — very cold. The mercury frequently fell to 25 degrees below zero Fahrenheit, and often stayed below freezing point for days at a time. The ground froze to a depth of a foot or more, and ice on the Imjin River was thick enough to support traffic. This suited the Canadians in particular, as they were able to indulge in their favourite sport of ice hockey. There was very little snow, which only appeared on the warmer days.

Our tents were heated by pot-bellied stoves fueled by Diesel oil. The 44- gallon drum was placed outside the tent and the oil piped into the stove through a copper tube, which had a control valve near the stove so that the oil flow could be regulated. One really cold days we kept the valve wide open, and the first two sections of the stove pipe would be glowing red. It's a marvel that the tent roof never caught fire.

For safety reasons we were not allowed to keep the stove burning all night, so by morning there was a coating of frost on the walls and ceiling. Our boots were often frozen to the dirt floor, and had to be freed by a sharp rap with a rifle butt. It took a strong effort of will to force oneself to emerge from the warmth of the sleeping bag on those bitter mornings!

Before the end of his shift at 0600hrs it was the custom for the prowling guard to go around the camp and light all the stoves, so that we were able to heat a mess tin of water for a bit of a wash and shave before parade. It was our practice to fill the mess tin at night and leave it on the locker, where it would be frozen solid by morning.

By the time cold weather set in in earnest, we had received all our winter gear, and it has to be said that the British clothing and equipment was at least the equal of that supplied to any of our allies, including the Americans. We had special insoles which insulated the feet from direct contact with the cold boot soles, and helped prevent frostbite. There were heavy flannel "long johns" and knitted string vests, which were particularly effective. The trick with these was to wear the string vest next to the skin, and put on an ordinary singlet over it, thus creating hundreds of air pockets that provided excellent insulation. We were issued with three-ply gabardine trousers and jackets which were shower- and wind-proof, and to top it all, a truly splendid garment, the parka. This was a thigh-length hooded jacket, made of three-ply gabardine, and was fleece-lined. Inside the rim of the hood was a malleable wire, which could be bent into shape so as to form a slit that left only the eyes visible, much like the visor of a knight's helmet. This was very useful — not only did it protect the face and ears from the icy wind, but also prevented the inspecting officer from seeing clearly whether you had had a shave or not!

Parkas were very expensive — they cost 15 pounds each, about a month's pay for a three-star Gunner, and that was the sum deducted from the pay of anyone who lost, destroyed, or sold his parka on the black market, and found that deep into the winter he really needed a replacement. I would love to have been able to keep my parka for later use when I returned to civilian life, but when spring arrived all our parkas were taken from us, presumably to be sent off for cleaning and storing for re- issue the following winter.

It was necessary to wear our woollen gloves outside, partic- ularly when handling a rifle or a shovel, or anything else with metal parts for that matter, otherwise the bare flesh would stick to the metal and take the skin off— very painful, and possibly causing a risk of infection.

We were fortunate enough to be well equipped against the rigours of the harsh climate, but I did feel for our predecessors, especially those who had served during the winter of 1950-1. At that time they were not nearly as well equipped as we now were, and moreover were on the move for much of the time. It must have been hell for them.

By contrast we had as easy a time of it as conditions permitted. We still had parades of course, and regular training sessions, as much to keep our minds from stultifying, I think, as for any practical purpose. Guard duties were a constant curse — more irksome and uncomfortable than ever at this time of the year! Once again our officers were very decent about it — we even had a paraffn stove in the sentry box at the camp entrance, and the prowler spent very little time actually prowling!

The camp still had to be maintained in good order, and we were expected to keep the tents and ourselves as neat and tidy as conditions permitted. The officers were kept busy thinking up jobs for us to keep us from all going troppo! One of the jobs that I got involved in was painting the interior of the Command Post truck, which had been judged to be in need of refurbishment. My partner for the enterprise was one of the minority of regular gunners among us, a Geordie who had raised the technique of skiving to an art form.

We were given a tin of cream paint and a couple of brushes, and left to get on with it. The first thing we did was to slap some paint on the front wall, and then decided it was time for a snooze. The truck was equipped with a sturdy fold-out shelf on each side. When in use the shelves carried the radios, telephones, charts etc. which were the tools of our trade. The back door of the truck, the only access to the work area, could be barred from the inside, so having secured the bolts to ensure that nobody could take us by surprise, we settled down for a nap. As the work progressed, of course, the shelves also had to be painted. We did them one at a time, so that there was always one free for use as a bunk. We took turns at sleeping on the floor when one of the shelves was thus unavailable.

This became our routine daily pattern thereafter — an hour or so of work, and the rest of the day spent in sleeping, broken by lunch and NAAFI breaks, and an occasional wander around camp to stretch our legs. When the bombardier in charge of the project queried why we had the door locked, Geordie explained that we were afraid that someone might burst in and cause us to spill the paint, or otherwise spoil our work.

Whenever the NCO asked how much longer we thought the job would take, Geordie would come up with an excuse about some difficulty we had struck in achieving good coverage on one area or another, or we had to wait for the undercoat to dry properly before we could apply the next coat. He was so plausible that I almost believed him myself. The upshot of it was that we squandered a couple of weeks on a job that should have been done in two days. To be honest I think the reason we were not harried into a more lively performance was because there really wasn't anything else to be done urgently, so leaving us alone saved the authorities the trouble of inventing more tasks!

On another occasion, in the middle of the winter, one of the junior officers decided that it was time we had a new latrine. From the stores the Kims and I drew a pick and shovel, and from the P.O.L. a 5-gallon drum of petrol. On arrival at the site, the first job was to dismantle the canvas shelter which protected the two-seater wooden "thunderbox" from the elements, and then move the thunderbox itself out of the way, exposing the half-filled trench. The scheme was to dig a new trench alongside the old one, so that the soil from the new pit could be thrown into the old one to fill it in without double handling. In the interests of hygiene we poured a little of the petrol into the old trench and set light to it. Then, under my instructions, the Kims scratched into the iron-hard ground the outline of the new trench, and poured some fuel over the marked area. The trench was to be about two feet wide by five feet long, and to a depth of six feet or so. I threw a match on the petrol-soaked ground, and we stood back until the flames died down. The soil was by now thawed enough for digging to commence. Kimshi swung the pick, and as soon as the soil was loosened and the air got to it there was a minor explosion as the petrol that had seeped into the ground ignited with a roar. So we gave it a few more minutes, then tried again — with more success this time.

Between them the Kims picked and scratched away the top layer of soil to a depth of two or three inches, which was as far as it had thawed. After alternate petrol treatments and diggings, we got through the frozen soil and the work became much easier. The Kims took turns at digging and resting, and the trench gradually got deeper as the old one slowly filled up. As they got deeper and deeper they began to disappear from sight, and all that could be seen was shovelful after shovelful of dirt arcing with great accuracy from one pit to the other. At this stage they had to dig footholds in the side of the trench in order to climb out to change shifts. It was slow work, but eventually the trench had reached a depth that I thought was enough to satisfy the bombardier, so I got the Kims to level and stamp down the soil over the old trench, and we carefully manoeuvred the thunderbox into position over the new one.

All that was left was to erect and securely anchor the canvas shelter, and the job was done. By now it was early afternoon, so I thought it was prudent to delay returning the tools to the store in case somebody spotted us and decided to find us another job. A smoke in the shelter of our new edifice seemed to be a sensible idea, so we retired there and sat gossiping for an hour or so. Every so often I emerged to make sure we were not attracting any attention, but all was quiet. We stayed until I thought it was safe to report the completion of our mission to the bombardier, who having inspected the work, pronounced himself satisfied and we were dismissed.

This same officer was full of bright ideas, and another of his brainwaves was to experiment with an American practice he had heard about, which they called "bitching sessions." At these the rabble were invited to raise any matters concerning morale. They could speak freely, without fear of recrimination, and where possible remedial action would be taken.

At the first such meeting I brought up the question of getting to the shower point at Div. H.Q. since the primitive shower arrangements in the camp were not in operation during winter. It was, I said, like pulling an eye tooth to obtain transport for this purpose. Stung by my remarks, the officer, as a demonstration of good faith, organised a jeep and driver for me that very afternoon, stipulating only that I should obtain from the attendant there written confirmation that I had been afforded the luxury of a hot shower.

The driver and I had a good skive for the rest of the day, and the following morning, when the officer demanded to see my note from the shower attendant, I came over all indignant and said "Sir, you couldn't expect me to ask him for a note — he would think I was a manky bastard who had to be compelled to have a shower!"

He thought about it for a few moments, and having obviously concluded that I had a point, he muttered a few words about obeying orders and walked off in a bit of a huff. The outcome was that there were no more "bitching sessions"!

In this way we passed our time through the long, bitter winter. We were not actually in hibernation, but for much of the time we might as well have been. November stretched into December, and Christmas and New Year came and went without much fanfare. The usual Army traditions were observed — on Christmas Day, as far as possible, all essential duties were performed by Scotsmen, so that they would be free for the New Year celebrations, but it didn't really make much difference in our situation as there was little enough to celebrate in any case.

In accordance with time-honoured practice Christmas dinner was served to us by the officers, some of whom looked a bit uncomfortable in the role of waiter! We also received a tot of rum, an Army tradition known in the Artillery as "gunfire. Unlike our cousins in the Royal Navy, we were not given the rum neat — instead the duty officer poured a generous measure into each man's mug of strong Army tea.

14

THE C.A.T.C

Towards the end of February I received a pleasant surprise — I was selected to attend the next course at the Commonwealth Artillery Training Centre. Why me, I thought — surely I was not being rewarded for my long and meritorious service? More likely the C.O. reasoned that I was the one who would be missed the least!

Anyway, I was very excited about it — I had heard from others who had been on the course that it was an interesting experience, and not only did it use up a considerable amount of your service time, but was in itself a good skive. The course was of six weeks' duration, and would end with a passing out examination to prove to our unit commanders that we had not been wasting everybody's time.

The Centre was housed in the buildings of what in calmer times had been an agricultural college, to which function it would presumably revert eventually. The courses catered for members of all the Commonwealth Artillery regiments then serving in Korea, so there were Gunners from Britain, Canada and New Zealand.

There were separate courses for gun crews, surveyors, and the one I was to join, which was the Technical Assistant R.A. class, the nearest thing to C.B.O Assistant that was available at the Centre. The other members of the class had an advantage over me because they had all worked as TARAs, while I was the only one who had been a C.B.O. Ack.

Among the skills we would be learning was how to set up and use the Artillery Board, or Arty board as it was known. The board was essentially a blank map. A swivel pin representing the No. I gun was pinned on the board, and on this was mounted an arm marked in yards. At the end of the arm there was an arc marked in degrees showing the bearing from the gun position. Then, using the information provided by the observation posts, it was possible to pinpoint with reasonable accuracy the position of the enemy gun. The bearing could be plotted easily enough from the OP's data. The distance was a bit more difficult, but an experienced OP operator could give a pretty accurate estimate, perhaps by the sound-ranging method, known as "flash to bang", where the distance could be gauged by the time lapse between the flash from the gun barrel and the sound of the gun being fired. Of course it helped the TARA greatly if there were reports from two OPs.

There were a number of factors to be taken into account before accurate data could be relayed by the TARA to the gun-layer. I had not realised how complicated it could be, and my respect for these people increased immensely. Intricacies of factors such as wind speed and direction, atmospheric conditions and temperature and so forth had all to be taken into account.

As well as a thorough grounding in the duties of a TARA we were given an insight into the surveyor's art. Among other things each of us had a go at setting up a theodolite and staff. We were also required to calibrate our pace. The way this was done was by walking at a normal pace along a measured 100 yard track, and counting how many paces it took to cover the distance. Each of us had to do this two or three times to ensure that we were pacing consistently. I found that it took me 110 paces from end to end each time I tried

This exercise brought to mind the origin of our word "mile." It is derived from the Latin "mille", a thousand, as in "mille passus", or a thousand paces, this being a standard Roman measurement probably originating with the Roman legions. When I first heard this I was a bit puzzled, because it was known that the Romans were on average shorter than people nowadays, and so a thousand of the legionary's paces would have been closer to half a mile than to a mile, and it is accepted that the Roman mile was about 1610 yards.

When I learned that "mille passus" meant a thousand double paces, the picture became clearer. I offer this fairly useless information for the diversion of anyone remotely interested in collecting trivia.

The C.A.T.C. was located not far from the small town of Yong Dong PO, and at weekends we were for the first time able to make the acquaintance of Koreans of all ages and both sexes, not just males of our own age. The people were for the most part friendly and hospitable, but it was very sad to see the abject poverty they lived in. It was not easy to get them to pose for photographs, especially the older folk.

Apparently they had a superstition that pictures took away part of the soul. On one of our forays into the town we were treated to the spectacle of a convoy of trucks heading south. As they approached we saw that they were loaded, standing room only, with cheering, shouting, laughing, flag-waving Chinese. They were ex-POWs on their way to join Chiang Kai-Shek's Nationalist forces on the island of Formosa (now Taiwan), to which Chiang and the remains of his army had retired after their defeat by Mao's victorious People's Army in 1949. I have no idea where these people had been, or what they had been doing for the last four or five months. I had understood that most of the ex-POWs of both sides had been repatriated long ago.

It was said that altogether about 17,000 Chinese POWs had elected to join Chiang rather than to return to mainland China, and that number no doubt included the ones we saw at Yong Dong PO. It is possible that many of them had relatives already in Formosa. Perhaps also some of them feared that they might be treated with great suspicion if they returned to the People's Republic — they had after all been exposed for a long spell to the corrosive effects of Capitalist contamination!

I have never seen any data relating to the North Korean POWs, or how many of them may have remained in the South, but it is a fair bet that there would have been a significant number of defectors among them as well.

All too soon the six week holiday was over. We had all reached at least a satisfactory pass standard in the examination, so there were congratulations all round, and a rousing celebration followed before we dispersed to our units. There were naturally widespread regrets that the course was finished, for it had indeed been a most enjoyable experience among a very congenial group of people, and a welcome break from the dull routine at CB Troop.

15

DIVERSIONS

Back "home" life resumed its normal course, with the officers racking their brains to invent things for us to do. As spring arrived and the weather began to improve, one of the 2nd. Lieutenants, who was kind of fitness fanatic, conceived a novel diversion for us. He decided it would be a great idea for us to rise at 0600 hrs and jog the mile or so to the river beach for an early morning swim, followed by a bout of calisthenics before jogging back to camp for breakfast. As some sort of compensation for disturbing our slumber at the crack of dawn, he arranged for us to receive a shot of "gunfire" before we set off, and that relieved the pain somewhat.

One day I read in the Stars and Stripes that the Van Doos were due to return to Canada in the very near future, so I decided that I would go and see my old mate Marcel before they left. It was much easier by this time to get around and visit friends in other units, for travel restrictions had been greatly relaxed. Even the most pessimistic had come to accept that the cease fire was real, and was likely to hold, so the danger of a sudden enemy assault was much reduced. So as long as you had the time, and could get out on to the MSR, you could thumb lifts to almost anywhere.

So the next Sunday afternoon I set off, and having hitch-hiked in a couple of stages, arrived at the Vandoo camp in time for the evening meal. I soon tracked Marcel down — he was obviously well-known and popular among his comrades — and our reunion was a joyous one.

My presence was not questioned by the kitchen staff — it was common enough in these ceasefire days for unexpected guests from other units to appear, especially at weekends, and I was able to enjoy an excellent feed in good company. Despite the antipathy often felt by French Canadians towards English-speaking people, this feeling fortunately did not always extend to personal relationships.

After the meal we made our way, with a group of Marcel's friends, to the wet canteen. Here, over the next several hours, we consumed a good deal more of the amber fluid than was perhaps advisable. The Canucks were of course in high spirits to begin with since they were so close to going home, and they were by nature hospitable, even to a Limey!

The carousing naturally included the singing of many French Canadian folk songs, most of which were unfamiliar to me. I did join in one though — the old favourite "Alouette", which was well known the world over.

I had originally planned to get back to CB Troop later that evening, but that turned out to be impossible, not only because I was not in a fit state to travel due to excessive intoxication, but also because the Pintail Bridge, which I would have to cross, was closed to all but essential traffic from 2359hrs until early morning, and it was well after midnight before I had given a thought to leaving. So when the party eventually broke up, there was nothing for it but for Marcel to scare me up a sleeping bag for what was left of the night. At last we staggered back to the tent, and I collapsed on to the sleeping bag in a drunken stupor.

The next morning I woke with a thumping headache and a

mouth that tasted much like I imagine the bottom of a parrot cage would. After a splash of cold water to clear my fuzzy head I managed a pretty good breakfast, and felt a bit more human.

Then there were the heartfelt goodbyes and good wishes for the future, and it was time for me to be off. Marcel commandeered a Jeep and gave me a lift to the MSR, where we bid a last farewell and I set off to hitch a ride home. It must have been after nine o'clock by then, so it was about ten a.m. when I finally staggered into camp. Before I had even reached the tent I was hailed by one of the NCOs, who informed me with unseemly glee that I was being put on a fizzer for being AWOL. Fortunately I had not been absent for long enough to be classed as a deserter, a much more serious offence. As soon as he heard that I was back, the BSM took charge of the situation, and I was marched off to the guardroom.

In due course I was submitted to the humiliation of shedding my cap and belt, and being marched at the double between my two escorts into the office to face the C.O., who was to hear the case. I was very fortunate in many ways, because we had quite recently acquired a new C.O. Our old one had been a real martinet from whom one could expect to receive the maximum sentence, while the new bloke was of a totally different stamp. He was a quiet, mild-mannered sort of fellow — a serious, no doubt competent and conscientious officer, who sometimes had a faraway, meditative look, as though his mind was elsewhere. He had a kindly, almost fatherly disposition. I judged him to be nearing retirement age, and so past the stage of seeking advancement by being overly regimental.

On the way to the office the BSM had been regaling me with details of his expectations regarding my probable punishment.

At least a month in the glasshouse, he predicted with an evil smirk. From what I knew of the C.O. I was rather less pessimistic than that, but you could never tell in these cases.

He had my charge sheet in front of him, from which he gravely read me the details of the alleged crime, and asked me what I had to say in my defence. There wasn't much I could say really, since I had obviously been absent when I shouldn't have been. So I mumbled something about having been to a farewell party for an old friend at the Vandoos' camp, and had been overcome by the occasion.

He gave me a bit of a lecture about my responsibilities, reminding me that I was still on active service, and was expected to behave accordingly. His manner was so grave and his expression so stern that I feared that the worst was about to descend upon me.

As he came to the point of delivering his verdict the mood seemed to change. He remarked that hitherto my record, while not having set the world alight, had been free of any serious blemish, and he was mindful that I had been here for quite a long time, almost a year in fact. Therefore, he said, he was inclined to view the case with a degree of leniency. He then pronounced the magic words "Case admonished", which meant that while I had received a verbal reprimand, there would be no further penalty.

I heaved a huge, silent sigh of relief as the BSM angrily marched me out. He was bitterly disappointed that I had escaped so lightly. The only thing he could think of to ease his wrath was to roar at me to "get a haircut." I scuttled off at high speed, gathering up my hat and belt as I fled, before he could gather his wits enough to dream up any more indignities to heap upon me. I was careful to stay out of his way for a few days afterwards.

16

KAMAKSAN

As part of the plan to mitigate the effects on morale of our mind-numbing boredom, one of the lieutenants came up with the idea that a day in the countryside would do us good. He arranged for the occupants of our tent, twelve in number, to go on an orientation expedition. After morning parade he demonstrated that his organisational skills had been at work. We picked up our haversack rations from the mess hall and stowed them in our small packs. He made sure we all had full water bottles, then we were split into pairs and got aboard the three-tonner he had laid on.

The idea was that we would travel about twenty miles to the south, where we would be given a map of the district, and then we would be dropped off, a pair at a time, at various points far enough apart so that no two pairs were in sight of each other. We were given a set of co-ordinates denoting the rendezvous at which we were to gather. My partner for the exercise was a good mate of mine called Dave Marshall. He was generally referred to as Big Dave, for he stood about six feet two and weighed at least thirteen stone. Like many big men, he was a good-natured, easy-going bloke. He came from somewhere in the Home Counties, Surrey I think.

After dismounting from the truck, we studied our map for a while, without becoming much wiser about our location, for neither of us was an accomplished map- reader. We did manage to work out from the co-ordinates we had been given that our destination was the top of the highest hill in the area covered by the map, a hill known as Kamaksan. This knowledge was of limited value to us, however, because we had only a sketchy idea of our exact position relative to the hill in question. Moreover the surrounding hills all looked very much the same height. After deliberating for several unproductive minutes we spied in the distance a white-clad figure that we thought must be a Korean peasant working in a paddy field. He was the only other human being in sight, so we made our way towards him in the hope that he might understand enough English to be able to help us.

The paddy fields were divided by banks, or dykes, along which we able to proceed without getting our feet wet. This was as well, given the Korean practice of using human waste as fertiliser!

When we reached the farmer, a wizened, weather- beaten old fellow with a wrinkled face and no teeth, we opened negotiations by offering him a cigarette which he accepted with many nods and smiles, satisfied now that we meant him no harm. As expected, we found that his English was rudimentary, but at the mention of the carefully enunciated name "Kamaksan" his face lit up, and with many an excited gesture and a flood of, to us, unintelligible babble, he finally pointed out our target, which we now saw was indeed the dominant feature of the range of hills. As a reward for his help I gave him a handful of cigarettes, which he eagerly pocketed, and we parted on excellent terms!

Confident now, Dave and I set off at a brisk pace, and were soon out of the paddy fields and in the lower slopes of Kamaksan. The terrain was rougher here, rocky and with scrubby vegetation. The hill was quite steep, making me realise once again how lucky I was to have arrived in Korea so close to the end of hostilities.

We took the climb in stages, stopping a couple of times to catch our breath, and at last reached the top of the hill, from where we had a panoramic view of the countryside. None of the others was in sight — the advantage we had gained courtesy of the old peasant meant that we were well ahead of the field.

After we had had a rest, Dave and I wandered about as we waited for the rest to arrive. In a bit of a depression in the ground I came upon a few bones. I called Dave over, and we continued to fossick around, turning up more and more bones. Although we had little knowledge of anatomy, we agreed that the bones looked very much like human ones. There was no skull, but there were many others, some of which were apparently leg and arm bones, and others that we thought looked like ribs. They were bleached, and one or two seemed to have been broken. The bones were scattered about, and I gave as my opinion that they had probably been disturbed by a pack of wild dogs, or perhaps wild pigs. They had obviously been there for a long time, and some of them were half buried. We gathered up as many of the remains as we could, and arranged them in some sort of order, leaving gaps for those that were missing.

As well as the bones there were a few scraps of faded cloth, which we thought had been part of a uniform, and some bits of what looked like webbing equipment. Amidst the debris I spotted a small leather pouch, of the kind used to carry a compass, with a loop at the back to fit on a belt. The leather was dry and cracked, but still intact. I opened it very' gingerly, and inside found not a compass, but two small wooden blocks. They were about three quarters of an inch square and perhaps two inches long. I carefully removed them from the pouch, and found that on one end of each were carved in minute detail what I took for Korean characters, though of course I couldn't identify them. I replaced the blocks in the pouch, and put it in my pocket for future investigation.

When we got back to our vantage point on the hilltop we could see others struggling up the slopes from all directions, and before long the whole company was assembled. Having accomplished our mission, we all broke out our haversack rations and settled down for a leisurely lunch. We had not brought any tea with us, as it was a warm day, and we managed well enough with our water bottles.

For this exercise we had been provided with proper sandwiches, rather than the hard-tack biscuits that were sometimes issued on field exercises. The hard-tacks were well named, for it required strong teeth to deal with them. They were about the size of ordinary cracker biscuits, but very, very much harder. They had a glazed surface, which made them impervious to water and, I'm sure, absolutely weevil-proof. If you broke a bit off and put a match to the broken end, it would catch fire and burn with a blue flame. They were quite filling though, and went well with a bit of butter and cheese.

Another example of Army ingenuity was the self-heating tin of soup or other liquids like chocolate milk. The tin had a hollow centre filled with some sort of solid flammable substance, which could be lit with a match or lighter. By the time this had burned out the contents of the tin were brought to a pretty high temperature. It was wise to remember to punch a hole in the top of the tin before lighting the fuel element, or the whole thing might blow up in your face! These items were issued mainly in the colder weather of course, and only sparingly then. I suspect that like so much else of our stores, they were surplus goods from 1945!

After we had finished lunch we sat around for a while enjoying the warm afternoon sunshine, as we waited for the truck to appear on the road below. The following day I sought out Kimshi and showed him the wooden blocks I had found, and asked him what he made of them. He got a bar of soap, on which he pressed the carved ends and was then able to decipher the characters. He said that the stamps, for such they were, showed the rank, name and unit of a company commander of the ROKA. I told him that I had found the pouch near the top of Kamaksan, and that there was a partial skeleton there as well. At this he became quite excited, and pressed me for more details. I described to him as best as I could the exact location of the remains. He became more and more agitated, and said that at the first opportunity he intended to take Kim On Ha with him to the site I had described in order to give the remains a proper burial — I had gathered previously that the Koreans in general set great store by the solemn observance of respect for the dead.

He asked me if he could keep the stamps so that he could try to get more information on the dead man from the Korean army authorities, and also see if he could trace any surviving members of the deceased man's family. If successful, he would give them the stamps as a memento. I had intended to keep the stamps myself as an unusual souvenir, but moved by Kimshi's appeal, I willingly surrendered them to him. I never heard whether or not his efforts had borne fruit, but it is to be hoped that he was successful.

17

ENTERTAINMENT

Every so often one of the larger units would take pity on us, and invite a party of us to share whatever entertainment they had laid on. It might be a visiting Concert Party like the one that featured so hilariously, to the disgust of Sarn't Major Sahib, in the television comedy "It ain't 'alf 'ot Mum." More often it would be a film show.

The occasion that sticks most vividly in my mind was the showing at the Canadian Artillery camp of the recently released film "Calamity Jane", starring Howard Keel and Doris Day. At this time Doris Day was very popular, a Forces' Favourite really, and I'm sure the object of many a fantasy among the lonely and deprived soldiery. For many years afterwards, whenever I heard the hit song from the film, "Secret Love", I was transported back to that memorable evening.

Not only was the film thoroughly enjoyable, but there was also a newsreel, one of the items of which dealt with the arrival back in Quebec City of the Vandoo battalion, and lo and behold, there on centre stage, none other than my old friend Marcel Frechette, embracing an elderly woman, presumably his mother. It was an eerie feeling, seeing him like that, and a pleasant reminder of the good times at Britannia Camp.

Another event occurred that evening, on the way back to CB Troop that made the outing unforgettable. For some time I had been suffering from a series of boils, one after another, on different parts of my body. I was not the only one so afflicted several of my comrades also complained of the same problem. It was generally assumed that the outbreak was the result of the absence of fresh fruit and vegetables in our diet over an extended period.

Anyway, at the time of the Secret Love trip I had a very painful boil in the groin. It was nearly on the point of bursting, and was quite sensitive. When the show was over, I was one of the first to board the three-tonner for the homeward journey. I sat on the floor of the truck, with my back braced against the side so as to provide some stability. As the truck filled up, several of the blokes had to stand, clinging to the steel framework of the canopy. One of these was Big Dave, who was right in front of me.

All went well for a while, until suddenly the truck lurched as the driver swerved to avoid a pothole or something, and Dave lost his balance, fell and landed fair and square in my lap. The agony as my boil erupted with the impact of his weight was so intense that it caused an adrenalin rush, giving me supernatural strength.

Despite the fact that Dave outweighed me by about three and a half stone, I hurled him off me with such force that he cracked his head on the steel frame, and collapsed in a heap on the floor.

The incident rather strained relations between Dave and me — we were both in some discomfort — but when we got back to camp, and I had cleaned up the mess made by the burst boil, and Dave's head had ceased throbbing, all was forgiven, and the normal relationship restored.

There was a source of relief open to those who were feeling the strain of isolation and deprivation, and that was the five days' leave in Tokyo known as R&R, or Rest and Recuperation. In the beginning R&R Was designed to provide a much needed rest for battle - weary troops, but in the more peaceful atmosphere of the post- cease fire days, it had become more of a break to relieve the debilitating boredom.

The leave was available to anyone who had spent a year or so in Korea and felt they could do with a change of scenery. I never myself took advantage of the opportunity — somehow I never seemed to have saved enough of my pay to make it worthwhile. But for most of the people I talked to who had been to, Tokyo it seemed to have been a barely remembered orgy of drunkenness and debauchery. I gathered that as soon as the plane touched down in Tokyo it would be met by a bevy of beautiful girls, each trying to latch on to one of the soldiers, offering to be a willing companion for the duration of his leave, and promising all manner of delights. They would go to an inexpensive hotel, which would be their base of operations for the period. The girls would act as tour guides during the daylight hours, and the nights would take care of themselves.

At the end of the five days the revellers would return to Korea, often feeling rather fragile, with fuzzy heads and empty pockets. It was not unusual for one or two of these lads to be carrying a "social disease", requiring painful and generally unsympathetic treatment from the M. O.

Sometimes one of the blokes would fall hopelessly in love with his Japanese paramour, who would of course assure him of her undying devotion. This too could be painful for the lover. One of the blokes in our tent fell into the trap, and on his return, despite warnings from his mates that his girlfriend was at that very moment probably entertaining another "lover", wrote many passionate letters, one or two of which were answered, before inevitably the replies stopped, and his began to be returned unopened. He was naturally devastated by the turn of events, which to him was as distressing as receiving a "Dear John" letter.

Because of its nature, R&R was often referred to as "Rack and Ruin", or more colourfully, as in the forthright American expression, as "A&A", standing for Alcohol & Ass, the latter being a synonym for sex. With our customary reserve and feel for decorum, we British were more likely to refer to "I&I", or "Intoxication and Intercourse"!

Although I never sampled the delights of Tokyo, I did have a few days' leave at the Division's rest camp near Inchon. This was a very comfortable resort, luxurious compared to CB Troop. I enjoyed a few relaxing days there, met a lot of interesting people from various units, and was able to get into Seoul once or twice to see my old mate Wayne Messick, who was at the time auditioning potential new members for USO concert parties.

18

THE SHOOT

The day of the great Commonwealth Divisional Artillery Shoot dawned clear and warm, promising ideal conditions for the event. All the Artillery units were to take part in the exercise, which was expected to last most of the day. There were regiments representing all three Commonwealth nations involved, Britain, Canada and New Zealand, so there would be some fierce rivalry.

Because there would be no enemy guns to be located and identified, CB Troop's participation in the actual manoeuvres was not required, so we were allocated another task — we were to provide personnel to man the pickets, which would be posted at the junctions with the MSR of all the roads leading into the target area. The idea of this precaution was to prevent unauthorised people from entering the danger zone, and possibly being annihilated by what our American allies are wont to describe, euphemistically, as 'friendly fire." A curious term when you think about it — I find it difficult to imagine a less friendly act than blowing people to smithereens, even unintentionally!

The scheme was to post two men at each road junction, possibly to keep each other company, or perhaps for fear that a man on his own might fall asleep! My companion for the day was "Taffy" Williams, a good friend of mine, and incidentally the only Welshman in our Troop at the time.

We drew our haversack rations from the cookhouse — this

time the pack included a "dry brew", that is a packet of tea, some sugar, and a tin of Carnation evaporated milk. There was also a billy can in which to brew up; it was expected that we would find plenty of dry firewood lying about. We were not required to take our rifles on the trip, as it was felt that shooting would-be trespassers would rather defeat the purpose of our being there — our responsibilities would be confined to issuing a warning.

There were about a dozen of us in the detail, and as we boarded the truck we were in high spirits, for it promised to be a very enjoyable skive — a whole day in the country without an authority figure in sight! A rare luxury indeed.

On arrival at our area of responsibility, Taffy and I set about gathering a few piles of firewood, so that the only work we expected to do that day would be done with first thing. The traffic on the MSR was light — the odd jeep or truck went by with hardly a glance at us, though occasionally a vehicle would stop, probably out of curiosity, to ask if we were OK or needed a lift somewhere. We passed the morning quietly, chatting amiably and occasionally taking forty winks — though not at the same time of course — one of us had to Stay alert at all times to avoid being caught napping! For one thing there was always a faint chance that some junior officer out joyriding might come upon us.

As lunchtime approached we got a good fire going, broke out our haversack rations, and brewed a billy of strong, sweet tea to go with our doorstep sandwiches. After lunch I spent an engrossing hour watching a colony of ants struggling to carry breadcrumbs larger than themselves up the bank, and dragging them into their nest. Sometimes, if the crumb was just too big to go in the entrance of the nest, they would bite it into smaller bits that would fit. Their perseverance was phenomenal — they never gave up.

About three o'clock or so we spotted some vehicles approaching from the north. From the size of the dust cloud they were kicking up it looked as though it was a large convoy. We went to the edge of the junction to get a good look, and as the cavalcade got close we saw that there were a couple of jeeploads of MPs in the lead, followed by a huge, open limousine flying two flags, one of which was the UN banner, and the other the Canadian ensign. Another couple of jeeps brought up the rear.

The occupant of the limousine was the Prime Minister of Canada, Louis St. Laurent, accompanied by staff and/or bodyguards. I recognised him from pictures I had seen. He had apparently been on a visit to the Canadian infantry battalions. Taffy and I threw up a smart salute and were rewarded with a smile and a cheery wave, and then they were gone in a cloud of dust. Thus ended my brief brush with fame!

We had been able to hear the distant roar of the guns during the shoot, and when the firing stopped we knew that the truck would soon be along to pick us up, at the end of a very pleasant day.

At a later date I was talking to a Canadian friend, and mentioned having seen St. Laurent. He then told me a bit more about the PM. The story was that the young Louis had believed as a child that men spoke French, and women spoke English. This was because his father, a French-Canadian, naturally conversed in French with his friends, while his mother, who was of Scottish ancestry, spoke English with hers. Louis himself grew up fluently bi-lingual, which was no doubt of great advantage to him in his political career.

19

MORE DIVERSIONS

Not all breaks from the routine were as pleasant as the Artillery Shoot had been. One that was far less agreeable was the time I had to visit the dentist. One of my eye teeth had been bothering me for several weeks, but having heard horrifying tales of the insensitivity of Army dentists, I was determined to postpone the evil day for as long as possible, hoping in fact that I would be able to hold off until I was demobbed and could see a civilian dentist. This was not to be however, for the pain became intolerable, finally forcing my hand. It so happened that a tent-mate, a Cockney named Derek Roxby, was similarly afflicted, so we decided to go together for moral support.

The procedure was to report sick after morning parade, and wait for the first available transport to take us to the nearest dental unit, which was at Divisional Headquarters. No appointment was necessary — you just showed up and waited for your turn. It turned out that our driver for the expedition was another old friend, Pete Cornford.

By the time we got to Div. HQ it was close to NAAFI break, so Pete headed for the canteen while Roxby and I made our way towards the dental surgery, which was in the back of a truck like the one we used as a command post. Roxby won the toss to see which of us would go first, so off he went to the torture chamber and I went back to the jeep to wait for my turn.

It seemed like a long time, but eventually the truck door opened and Roxby staggered down the steps, one hand over his mouth and blood trickling through between his fingers. With the other he pointed over his shoulder to indicate that it was my turn to face the music. His appearance did very little to boost my spirits, but there was nothing to be gained by delay, so I steeled myself and entered the truck.

To my relief the dentist, a captain in the Dental Corps, was nothing like the Army stereotype. Rather, he was a pleasant looking, fresh-faced chap, with a friendly expression which gave me more confidence. His assistant, a corporal also appeared amiable enough as he directed me to the chair. The captain examined my teeth, and remarked to the corporal that I had a big mouth, which would be easy to work in. I thought that was a bit rude, but of course I was in no position to raise objections!

It transpired that the Army does not much favour filling teeth — perhaps on the premise that a filling might later fall out and have to be replaced, while extraction provided a permanent solution to the problem. So in went the needle, giving at least partial relief from the pain, and the struggle began.

The tooth was evidently deep-rooted, for the dentist was fairly sweating with the exertion as he twisted this way and that, until at last the root gave way, and he stood triumphant, holding the dripping tooth aloft. I too was sweating, and was very glad when the dentist had packed the bleeding gum with cotton wool, and I was allowed to stumble out into the fresh air. The ride back to camp was quite relaxed now that it was all over.

I still went to visit my friends at the Air Ground Liason team now and then. They too had a rotation system, so that occasionally one of the old hands left and a new bloke arrived. One of the new fellows introduced himself as D.M. Kirkland. I asked him what the M." stood for, and was surprised when he replied that that was it — that was his given name. I found that hard to believe, as I had never before heard of such a thing. However the other blokes confirmed his claim. It was not that he came from an unusually large family, where his parents had run out of suitable names — it was just that this was a quite normal practice in the good ole U.S. of A. A weird mob indeed!

As the summer wore on and my day of redemption grew closer, I was able to contemplate realistically the approach of the coveted Early Breakfast. It was the custom in the Army for the demobilisation of those whose time was up and the intake of the luckless new recruits to take place on the same day, always a Thursday. This meant in effect that the period of National Service was actually two days short of two years, or even three days if there was a leap year involved — also the last day the escapees were free to go as soon as breakfast was over and they had their final pay in their hands, all other formalities having been completed on the Wednesday, so that day didn't really count..

I think the purpose of the early breakfast was not only to clear decks in readiness to receive the new intake, but also to avoid unnecessarily depressing the recruits by forcing them to witness the jubilant departure of the old guard!

So by the middle of July, if anyone asked me how long I had to go, my cheerful reply would be something like "Two months, three days and an early breakfast!" Furthermore, over six weeks of that time would be taken up with a few days' holiday at the transit camp in Kure, followed by a leisurely sea voyage. Things were looking up at last!

The U.S. Marine Division that had been on our right flank had been withdrawn from the line, and their positions were now occupied by the 28th. ROKA Division. In the interests of good international relations, one of our lieutenants decided it would be a good idea for us to get to know our neighbours, so he arranged for a dozen or so of us to go on a trip to see what was happening over there. Right after parade he and his driver set off in his jeep, and the rest of us followed in the three- tonner. We travelled a fair way into the 28th's territory without seeing much sign of life, until we came to a pleasant area that seemed like an ideal spot for a picnic style meal later on at lunchtime. Meanwhile we split up into groups, and wandered off in different directions on a kind of a voyage of discovery, to see how the countryside compared with our own bailiwick, agreeing to meet back at the truck in time for the midday meal.

Big Dave and I stayed together, and after we had walked for a mile or so, we heard the sound of gunfire off to our right. We made our way through the scrub until we came to a large pond surrounded by boulders. The gunfire we had heard was caused by a couple of ROKA officers, who were firing their pistols into the water. The impact of the bullets stunned some of the fish, which floated to the surface and were easily gathered by the shooters. A lazy way of catching their lunch!

It had by now quite hot, Dave and I off and enjoyed a leisurely swim in the refreshingly cool water, and sunbathed for nearly an hour on the warm rocks. At last we dressed and headed back to the picnic site, where some of the others had the billy on the boil. Lunch over, we had a little siesta before returning to CB Troop. We hadn't really seen much of our neighbours, but we'd had a good day out anyway.

At about this time a friend who was going home presented me with an ancient wind-up HMV gramophone and about a dozen 78 rpm records, one of which — the prize one — was Doris Day's hit "Secret Love." This one, being by far the most popular, received much more playing time than any of the others, so much so that I don't even remember what was on the other side!

The gramophone, being of great age, had steel needles rather than the diamond styluses of the future, and the records had been subjected to rough treatment in their travels, with the result that the sound quality was not of the highest. But it was the best we had, and gave many hours of enjoyment just the same.

Whenever it was somebody's birthday, or when somebody was on the point of leaving, or sometimes for no particular reason at all, it was the custom to have a bit of a party in the tent, and on these occasions the HMV was dusted off and put to work.

One such evening, when festivities were at their height, I went over to the wet canteen to fetch a few more bottles, and on my return with the Asahi I met by a dreadful sight. On my bunk, where I had foolishly left it, was one of the records, broken into three or four pieces. In accordance with Murphy's Second Law, which states in essence that anything that can possibly go wrong will most certainly do so, the broken record had to be "Secret Love", and of course so it was.

It seemed that Big Dave, being even clumsier than usual as a result of having imbibed more beer than he was accustomed to, had overbalanced and sat heavily on my prized possession. Predictably I was more than a little miffed, and a few harsh words were uttered, but in the end there was nothing to be done about it — spilt milk etc. — so peace was restored with no further damage being done. I was consoled by the thought that I would going home, and would be leaving the gramophone and records behind anyway.

20

THE WOOLLEY SAGA

There was one more dramatic event during my last days at CB Troop, and that was the Woolley affair. One of the more recent arrivals was a tall, well-built Midlander named Woolley. Nobody seemed to know his first name, but since from his accent it was obvious he came from somewhere in the sphere of influence of Birmingham, he was always called "Brum." He was a taciturn sort of bloke, not really unfriendly, but not given to idle chit-chat or to making friends easily. He had the kind of wry, caustic sense of humour that I had often noticed in people from the Midlands, and which I found rather attractive. He was the type that it would be handy to have on your side if there was any trouble. I rather liked him.

The morning that the drama took place began like any other — the sun was shining, we were on the usual parade, which was being taken by one of the sergeants, a man who was best known for having a miserable temperament (someone said he had an ulcer, which might have been the reason for his dyspepsia). He also had an unfortunate habit of smirking when issuing a rebuke.

Woolley happened to be in the front rank on this occasion, and I was directly behind him. The sergeant stopped in front of him, and for some reason asked his name (they had not previously met), to which Brum replied "Woolley." "Woolley what?" said the sergeant. At this Woolley stepped out of the ranks and felled the sergeant with a mighty blow to the jaw. It happened so suddenly that it took everybody by surprise. The blokes either side of Woolley grabbed him by the arms to prevent him from doing any further damage, and as the sergeant scrambled to his feet, Woolley was placed under arrest.

The reason for Brum's extraordinary conduct later became known, and was explained thus. Unbeknown to many of us, it had become common in the U.K. for raw recruits to be referred to as "woolly bears" because of the rough, hairy texture of their brand new battle dress uniforms. Woolley's reaction had been the result of an unfortunate misunderstanding. The sergeant had meant him to reply "Woolley, Sergeant", while Woolley had thought he was being sarcastic. The smirk hadn't helped. At his trial Woolley was sentenced to four weeks' detention — a fairly lenient outcome for such a serious offence. It is likely that even he himself was somewhat relieved.

In the event this was not the end of the matter, for there was an unexpected sequel to the drama. Woolley returned to CB Troop after serving his sentence, apparently not very much affected or chastened by the experience. Things seemed to have returned to normal, until it was the same sergeant's turn to take the morning parade. As he came to Woolley, who was again in the front rank, the sergeant said something to him. I did not hear what was said, as I was some distance away this time, but the smirk was there again. Whatever it was that the sergeant had said, it evidently enraged Brum, and the earlier scenario was re-enacted, like the rerun of an old film. Once again Woolley stepped forward and fetched the sergeant another haymaker that sent him crashing again to the ground.

The inevitable followed — another arrest, another trial, and another sentence. To everyone's surprise the sentence was the same as on the previous occasion — four weeks' detention. It had been expected that this time there would be a court-martial, with a much harsher sentence, and quite probably a dishonourable discharge. It was generally agreed that Brum had been very lucky indeed.

By the time Brum was released following his second stretch I was well on my way to Japan, so I never learned what happened afterwards. I could only hope that the Army would by this time have realised that the two men were totally incompatible, and posted one or both of them to different units as far as possible away from each other!

21

HOMEWARD BOUND

When the long-awaited day of my departure from CB Troop finally came it seemed to happen very suddenly. It was the 25th of July 1954, a touch over fourteen months since I had arrived, though it seemed much longer. The place had been home to me for more than a year, and I have to admit that there were some regrets at leaving. There were six of us going at the same time, and we had been together for a long time, so were well known to each other. It was a happy bunch indeed that got aboard the 15cwt. that would take us to the railhead for the journey to Pusan. But we were also leaving behind other good friends, and there had to be a tinge of sadness at the farewells. In my case I knew too that I would miss the Kims, and wondered what would become of them in the uncertain future. However, we had had a few beers the night before, so we were feeling a bit seedy, and that helped to dull the pain!

On the way to the railhead we got the driver to stop at the Commonwealth Division monument beside the road at the 38th Parallel, and asked him to take a photograph of the six of us clustered around it. The monument was a pale blue block on which painted in white the Commonwealth crown and the legend "38th Parallel." Unfortunately the picture didn't turn out very well when we had it developed in Japan, but we all got a copy of it anyway. It would be nice to think that the monument still stands there, but I expect that it has disappeared long ago.

At the railhead there was already a large number of blokes from various units waiting for the train. They' stood around in groups, surrounded by their equipment, all like us in good humour, smoking and gossiping without a care in the world.

At last the rattletrap train clattered in and came to a wheezing halt. It was the same one that had brought us here, or one very like it. Korean trains were built for economy rather than comfort, but we all clambered eagerly aboard nevertheless.

The journey to Pusan was a long and uneventful affair, but we had our haversack rations to sustain us, and a few times the train stopped and gave us a chance to stretch our legs. There was not the feeling of uncertainty and anxiety that there had been on the northward journey — this time we knew exactly where we were going, and what lay at the end of the trip.

As we approached Pusan the train was travelling more slowly, and at one stage we passed the dreaded Detention Centre. Through the high barbed wire fence I could see a group of prisoners, and among them I could swear I recognised one of them — a bloke named Fred (I forget his last name), whom I had known at Woolwich and on the "Empire Pride", but had not seen since. I wondered what mischief he had been up to that had landed him here.

At the railway terminal there was the usual chaos, with people milling about shouting and gesticulating and officers running around in all directions, until finally some sort of order prevailed. Eventually we climbed aboard the waiting trucks and were taken to the docks, where we got our first sight of the good ship M.V. (H.M.T.) "Dilwarra." The (M.V.) stands for "motor vessel" which is used during times of civilian transport whereas (H.M.T.) stands for Her Majesty's Troop ship, which is during times of war.

The Dilwarra was a sister ship of the Duneira, which later featured in the film "The Duneira Boys." She was a much more prepossessing vessel than Empire pride had been, and when we got aboard and were directed to our quarters, we found that there was no comparison. There was not a sign of a hammock to be seen — instead there were tiered bunks with proper mattresses, a much better arrangement as far as we landlubbers were concerned.

Nor were we required to have our meals in the sleeping quarters, as there was a separate dining area. Although conditions were crowded, as one would expect on a troopship, the whole environment had more of a feel of a passenger liner, and less of a cattle boat, than that of the poor old Empire Pride. In fact there were actually civilian passengers that joined the ship in Hong Kong, as well as in Singapore — the families of the servicemen returning to the U.K. from the garrisons in those places.

All in all it promised to be a far more enjoyable voyage than the outward one, especially as it turned out that the ship was equipped with stabilisers, greatly adding to the level of comfort during the heavy weather that we encountered in some stages of the journey, particularly in the Indian Ocean.

The short hop from Pusan to Kure gave us a chance to get our bearings on the ship, and get to know some of our fellow passengers. We spent five days in the transit camp, most of the time taken up with re-kitting, documentation and so forth. The camp was very pleasant — good food and comfortable accommodation, and a wonderfully relaxed atmosphere. Curiously, the latrine facilities were out of character with the rest of the place — thunder boxes and buckets rather than Water Closets. The buckets were emptied daily by one of the Japanese workers, who became known to us as "Honey bucket Charlie" because he emptied the toilet buckets into a couple of huge vessels which he carried on a yoke over his shoulders. He would trot off with these, and it was assumed that he sold the contents to local farmers for use, in the typical manner, as fertiliser on their paddy fields.

Charlie was a cheerful, friendly sort of bloke, and had a habit of buttonholing the unwary, on whom he would practise his rudimentary English. This could be very trying, with the flies buzzing around the odoriferous vessels, but it was hard to get rid of him without hurting his feelings! He was one of the few friendly Japanese, many of whom seemed quite surly and resentful. If you chanced to be walking and your path crossed that of a Japanese, he would stop to let you pass. He would bow, and appear deferential and polite, but as you went by the hostility was almost palpable. Kure is not far from Nagasaki, which of course was the target of the second atomic bomb in 1945, and no doubt the memories were still raw.

Although we were treated very well by the authorities in the transit camp, they naturally had to make some pretence now and then of imposing a bit of discipline, so one day we were ordered out in full kit for a route march, under the command of a good-natured bombardier. We were supposed to be going on a five mile "bash", and marched out of the camp in good order. When we were out of sight of the camp we came upon the NAAFI roadhouse, whereupon the bombardier called us to a halt, telling us to fall out, and form up again outside the roadhouse in three quarters of an hour. This would get us back to camp in time that nobody would suspect we had not been marching the specified distance.

That was about the only serious attempt that was made to remind us that we were still in the service — except for the inevitable inoculations and vaccinations to protect us from any nasty bugs that we might pick up while on shore leave in the various ports of call on the way back to the U.K., and the usual documentation and administrative B.S. Otherwise we were very much left to our own devices.

There was a free shuttle service run by the camp bus at frequent intervals between 6p.m. and midnight — we were already preparing for Civvy Street thinking in terms of the twelve hour clock rather than the Army's preferred 24 hour version!

Most of us spent our evenings in Kure at the beautiful NAAFI-run facility known as the Kookaburra Club. They served excellent Australian beer there at duty-free prices; cigarettes were also very cheap, and we were still receiving our free issue of fifty a week from the Nuffield foundation, a privilege we enjoyed until we disembarked in Southampton. There were table tennis tables, dartboards and a billiard table, and a substantial feed could be had for a few shillings, so altogether a good night out was quite affordable.

In its wisdom the Army restricted the amount of money we were paid each week, so as to protect us from making absolute pigs of ourselves, and maybe going AWOL in the process. As it was we did ourselves enough damage! I still have a temporary pass issued for use while our pay books were held for documentation, and the photograph on it makes me look like a total wreck — it was taken in the morning following a particularly heavy night, when I was not really at my best!

22

WESTWARD HO!

The idyllic existence in Kure couldn't last forever of course, and all too soon it was time to board the Dilwarra again. We had been issued with brand-new jungle green trousers and jackets for the homeward journey, probably to present a favourable image to the natives when we were ashore, as well as to the civilians who would be joining the ship en route.

It was a fine body of men therefore that clambered up the gangway, kitbags over shoulders and joyful anticipation in hearts. We had left our webbing equipment behind, as well as our rifles, none of which would be of any further use to us.

Once on board everybody went to the same quarters as we had occupied on the trip from Pusan, and were soon comfortably settled in. I knew that there would be some chores that would be allocated to us for the voyage. Basically the ship's crew were responsible for keeping the top deck shipshape, while the tidiness and cleanliness below decks were up to us. This arrangement was no doubt as much to give us something to do as for any other reason.

I had been advised by an old hand that the best job aboard ship was swabbing the ablutions, or the heads as they were known by seafarers. This did not sound like a very attractive option, but my informant insisted that it was a really good skive, and because it wasn't a popular choice, it would be given to the first volunteers that applied. At my urging my good mate Dave "Brum" Whitehead joined me in stepping forward for the position, and sure enough we had no trouble in securing the job. We had already decided that we would team up as companions for shore leave etc. anyway, so it was natural to have the same duties on board.

We soon discovered that our choice had been a good one. All we had to do was to swill down the ablution block, which included hand basins, shower recesses, urinals and toilet cubicles — these last had no doors, which made the process easier still. We also had to make sure that there were plenty of toilet rolls and cakes of soap ready for use.

The soap was special stuff which yielded a weak, half-hearted sort of lather in the salt water that was used throughout the ablution facilities, where normal soap would have been ineffective. For the swilling down there was a large hose which provided a powerful jet, so that the process didn't take very long at all. As long as there were no complaints about our work we were left very much alone — no one really wanted to get involved, so there was no interference from anywhere.

We started our chores as soon as we had had breakfast and everybody else was busy about their own jobs, and most mornings our work was done well before ten o'clock, and we were enjoying the sunshine and sea air up on the top deck, which had by now dried out from the holy-stoning and hosing down which was the crew's daily routine.

The ports of call on the voyage westward were the same ones as on the way out, but in the reverse order of course! We dropped anchor in Hong Kong one morning soon after leaving Kure, and were allowed ashore for the afternoon, with orders to be back on board in time for the evening meal — the ever-cautious authorities were careful to ensure that we were not tempted to spend the night in the flesh-pots of the city! That first day Brum and I confined our activities to wandering about the streets, picking up the odd souvenir, and presents for the folks at home. The following day we were off again for the morning, and this time we took the funicular railway to the top of the island, the so-called Peak, from where we had a wonderful view of the harbour. It was a spectacular sight, and we could make out the Dilwarra at anchor far below.

On the Peak there were luxurious houses, the sumptuousness of which on the way down declined in direct proportion to the distance from the top. It was said that the richest white folks lived at the top, and the lower the descent on the slopes so the incomes of the residents fell. Next in order came the wealthy Chinese, and the same pattern applied until at last came the poorest of the population living on junks in the harbour.

We had intended to walk back down, in order to conserve our dwindling funds, but we found that the heat and humidity were more than we had bargained for, and we were soon sweating profusely. Fortunately we were rescued by a very nice middle-aged lady, who saw our plight and kindly gave us a lift in her huge limousine. And so we arrived back at the ship, tired, hungry, and very nearly broke, but happy nevertheless.

23

A NEW EXPERIENCE

It was after we set sail the following day that I found out that among those who had joined the ship in Hong Kong, both military and civilian, there was a young soldier who had suffered some kind of a mental breakdown and was being sent home as an invalid. I found this out because for some unspecified reason I was one of the first to be detailed to watch over the poor chap during the daytime. I suppose that because the patient happened to be a Gunner, it was natural that we of the Artillery persuasion were selected to be his companions — in this way he would feel himself to be among friends!

The plan was that during the waking hours there would be two of us on duty at a time, working in two-hour shifts, to look after him and make sure he didn't come to any harm. My partner for my first shift was a bloke from one of the regiments — I knew him by sight only, as we had never really met. We introduced ourselves, and tossed a coin to decide which of us would have the first hour in with the patient. We had been instructed that only one of us at a time was to sit with the patient in what I suppose could be called the day ward. Meanwhile the other would keep watch, through the heavily reinforced glass window in the steel door, which was locked from the outside, and would be ready to rush in to lend assistance if the patient became violent. Perhaps it was felt that the patient might be uncomfortable if there were two of us in the room with him, and that he might find a one-on-one situation less threatening.

I lost the toss, and it was with some trepidation that I entered the room to face the unknown. None of us had any idea of how to go about dealing with people who had any sort of mental illness, nor did we receive any help or advice from those above. In those days the Army did not consider it necessary to offer any counsel in such cases, beyond the usual instruction "Just do it!"

The room was equipped with a fixed table with a bench on either side, one of which was against the wall, or I should say, the bulkhead. Both benches were anchored to the floor, so there was no danger of them being used as a weapon — very reassuring!

In the event I had no cause for anxiety, for when the patient was ushered in I saw a fresh-faced, pleasant-looking bloke with no hint of aggression or threat about him. He was introduced as Tom, I gave him my name, and we shook hands, then sat at the table. In spite of the cordial greeting, I still sat with my back to the bulkhead, being a little cautious and uncertain until I saw how the land lay.

Our conversation began tentatively at first, but after a while the atmosphere more relaxed, and we were soon chatting amiably about our homes and families. It transpired that we had a lot in common, because we both had a farming background. Like me he was a West Country man — he was from somewhere in Somerset I think — so accent and dialect posed no problems! Once I had overcome my initial anxiety and doubts about my ability to handle the situation, I quite enjoyed Tom's company, and his attitude suggested that the feeling was mutual. Nor was this first meeting between us to be the last.

The following afternoon, while Brum and I were tusking in the warm sunshine on the top deck, our bombardier approached, and with the kind of evil grin that senior NCOs seem to reserve for occasions when they are delivering bad news to someone, said to me "Get yourself down below — your nutter mate wants to see you."

To see Tom's face light up when I appeared was reward enough for the inconvenience. This time he had brought with him some photographs of his family to show me. They looked like a typical farming family, posing self-consciously for the camera in front of their house, family dog lying obediently at their feet. There was also a picture of his girlfriend, an attractive girl with a shy smile. At that moment I sincerely hoped that in England he would receive the treatment he needed, and would make a complete recovery, for he appeared to have much to live for.

In the weeks that followed it became a regular pattern for Tom to send for me almost every day. I rather looked forward to these sessions, which often lasted a couple of hours. Sometimes we would play cards — not my favourite pastime, but Tom seemed to enjoy it and was quite good at it, regularly giving me a sound beating. At other times we would just sit and talk. He was an intelligent, sensitive fellow, obviously devoted to his family, and I could well imagine him tending the farm stock and working in the fields.

The day before we were due to dock in Singapore Tom asked me if I would be going ashore. When I replied that I certainly hope so, he asked me rather diffidently if I would do something for him. Of course I said I would, and he said he wanted very much to get a cheong-sam as a surprise gift for his girlfriend. I had had no experience of shopping for such items, but told Tom I would do my best to find what he wanted.

He then produced a wad of notes, far more than was needed, and brushed aside my protests and insisted that I take it all, "just in case." To get the right size would be a bit of a problem, I feared, but Tom reckoned that his girl came about up to his shoulder, and as I had a fair idea of her figure from her photograph, I thought I would probably be able to make an acceptable choice.

Brum and I went ashore together as usual, and strolled around the town making a purchase here and there from one or other of the many traders along the crowded streets, souvenirs for the family and so on. I decided I would leave the cheong-sam till we were on our way back to the ship — that would give me more time to check and compare prices and quality of the goods. All the traders, as expected, assured us that their stock was greatly superior to that of any of the others', earnestly advising us not to waste our money on the rubbish on offer by their competitors.

We made our way to the beautiful NAAFI-run Britannia Club where we enjoyed a few leisurely beers, and were sorely tempted to have a swim in the huge swimming pool. We were thwarted in the idea by not having swimming trunks with us, and we reasoned that appearing poolside in "drawers cellular", or worse still in the nude, as we had been able to do on the banks of the Imjin, would not perhaps be considered acceptable conduct in the present refined environment! It was a pity though, for Singapore can be uncomfortably warm and humid at that time of year, and a dip would have been more than welcome. Never mind, another cold beer or two provided fair compensation.

I enlisted Brum's assistance in selecting a very pretty cheong-sam, which, following protracted haggling with the shopkeeper, who did his best to break our hearts with his woeful tales of poverty and deprivation, and the difficulties of providing for a large family, did not after all make too big a hole in the funds Tom had provided. Then, having completed our own shopping, which had as usual been curtailed to a degree by the shortage of funds, Brum and I headed back to the Dilwarra well pleased with the excursion.

Tom was overjoyed when he saw what I had brought him — in fact his expressions of gratitude were so profuse as to be embarrassing, and he was further pleased, not to say surprised, by the amount of change I handed him.

On my next visit to Tom the day after we left Singapore, we were joined by another patient who had just come aboard. He was one of the very few soldiers in the British Army in those days from African descent, and the first that I had come across. In contrast to Tom, this fellow was taciturn, so uncommunicative that it was hard to get even his name out of him. He seemed moody and brooding, but as he displayed no sign of being dangerous, I did not feel unduly threatened. Besides having the guard outside the door, I felt that Tom would be on my side if the new bloke turned nasty! After a while the newcomer seemed to relax, and tentatively began to join in the conversation. He appeared quite friendly towards Tom, and thereafter I noticed that I was summoned less often than before.

24

COLOMBO CHARLIE

As soon as Brum and I set foot on the Colombo dockside we were accosted by a rickshaw driver who gave his name as Charlie (not another one, I thought — don't these people know any other English name?), and who assured us that he would take us all around the city on a sort of guided tour, for a very low charge. We told him we were together, but he insisted that there was no problem — there was plenty of room in the rickshaw for the two of us. So we agreed on a price for a couple of hours, squeezed into the ancient vehicle and set off on our tour of discovery.

Charlie was as good as his word — he took us to see some of the temples in the city, and the parks and other places of interest. He trotted tirelessly, and apparently effortlessly as he kept up a running commentary. His endurance was quite amazing for such a slight figure, and pulling a double load at that. We stopped a few times to take photographs, and Charlie was delighted when we included him in some of the shots.

At last it was time to return to the ship, so reluctantly we told Charlie to head for the docks. When we came in sight of the Dilwarra, Charlie took a sudden left turn into a side street, then right into another one, so that we lost sight of the dockside. Then he stopped, and as if by a pre-arranged signal, a sizeable crowd gathered around.

We had heard of occasions when a rickshaw driver had suddenly stopped and lifted the shafts up so that the passenger cracked his head on the road and was an easy target for robbery. We had not thought that Charlie was the type to try such a trick, but we swiftly hopped out anyway! However, we were ringed in by the mob, and could see no easy way out. Meanwhile Charlie demanded that we pay him twice the amount we had agreed, on the grounds that he had transported the two of us. He loudly proclaimed this argument to the crowd in their language, and there was a good deal of angry support for him from his countrymen. Brum and I made our resistance known quite forcefully, but that only served to increase the mob's wrath. We were not in a position to accede to Charlie's demands even had we wished to, because we had only set aside the agreed amount, and were otherwise penniless.

The situation was even worse than Jock and I had faced in Hong Kong so many months ago, for the Chinese crowd had only been sullen and quietly menacing, while this mob were shouting and gesticulating wildly, and appeared to be on the verge of violence. There was not a friendly face to be seen; Brum and I steeled ourselves for the impending onslaught, but were saved in the nick of time by the arrival out of nowhere of a local policeman. He had no doubt been attracted by the roars of the crowd, and had suspected what was happening. Intimidated by his presence, the mob dispersed into thin air as quickly as it had gathered. The policeman listened to both sides of the argument, and finally gave his verdict in our favour, much to Charlie's disgust and our relief. We were told to make ourselves scarce without delay, and we took this sound advice, legging it back to the safety of the Dilwarra in near record time.

I was extremely pleased that we had escaped so easily, because I had in my pocket an American silver dollar which had been given to me by a G.I. friend the year before, and which I had been guarding jealously ever since. At my request he had asked his mother to send the coin, which she had concealed in a pair of shoes she was sending him, it being frowned upon to send cash through the mail. As those who are familiar with the T. V. series M.A.S.H. will be aware, it was not unusual for American servicemen to have items of civilian attire, a practice which would not be tolerated in the British forces, certainly not the Army anyway.

I treated the silver dollar as a prized souvenir, and have it still. It would have been a severe disappointment to me to have lost it to Charlie if I had been searched! As a matter of mild interest, and yet another example of items in my fund of trivia, I learned many years later from a workmate who had spent some years in the Merchant Navy and had picked up many such tidbits of information, that the bald eagle featured on the silver dollar is shown looking over its right shoulder on coins minted in peacetime, while on those struck in time of war it faces to its left. When later that day I checked my dollar, which was minted in the peaceful year of 1921, I found that, lo and behold, the eagle is proudly looking to its right. Which all goes to show that not all seamen's tales need to be treated with suspicion!

25

THE HOME STRETCH

On the trip from Colombo to our last port of call, Aden, we were again subjected to some rough weather and heavy seas — the Arabian Sea seemed always to be hostile! But by now I was a seasoned sailor, and immune to the curse of seasickness, especially since the Dilwarra handled the conditions much better than the Empire Pride had done.

We had hitherto not even caught sight of the civilian passengers — they had been kept well quarantined from the ribaldry of the common soldiery. But now some of them suddenly appeared as the cast of a concert which they very kindly performed for our benefit. Surprisingly many of them were quite talented — or so it seemed to most of us, who had been starved of live entertainment for so long. There was a comedian, and others put on several amusing skits. One attractive blonde girl, of about our age I should think, gave a spirited rendition of a couple of popular songs. Her act was greeted by thunderous applause, stamping and whistling, and roaring demands for encore after encore. It was a treat to see and hear an English speaking girl after our long deprivation!

Aden was as unattractive as I remembered it from the previous visit, and I did little there but have a few drinks and send a postcard home. It had been my practice at every landfall to send a picture postcard to the family, with an account of our progress and an estimate of how much longer we would be at sea, and I still have some of them, which I recovered when I got home.

It was a tranquil cruise through the Red Sea after the buffeting we had received in the Arabian Sea, and then we passed through the Suez Canal and docked once more in Port Said. Again there was no shore leave, as the political atmosphere had worsened still further, even since our last visit, and so it was a brief stay only to pick up essentials for the run home.

We were relieved to sail again into the peace and quiet of the beautiful Mediterranean, this time heading in the right direction! The weather was warm and clear, the sea was calm, and every turn of the ship's propellers brought us nearer home — it was wonderful!

At last we sailed through the Straits of Gibraltar, and headed north. There was a bit more turbulence in the Atlantic, and especially once again in the Bay of Biscay, but it no longer mattered — we were on the home stretch! It was quieter through the Channel, and then, amid much jostling and cheering, we docked in Southampton. There was no band to greet us here, as there had been in Pusan fifteen months before, but still we were home.

There ensued the now familiar chaos of disembarkation, but it was more good- natured this time than on previous occasions. Joyfully we tramped down the gangway for the last time, and were finally assembled in our separate groups. We of the Royal Artillery' detachment marched off to board the train which would take us to our spiritual home at the Woolwich Depot.

When we arrived at the Depot we were allocated our quarters for the few days we still had to serve. During that time we would be weighed, measured, and medically examined to establish that no one was suffering from any ailment, disability, or disease that could possibly be attributed to our military service. As one might expect in the circumstances, the examinations were quite peremptory compared to the rigorous scrutiny that had attended those at our induction two years earlier. Clearly the Army was not keen to discover any problems that could be laid at its door! With the diabolical cunning for which it is renowned, the Army had ensured that the sergeant in charge of us was himself a Korean War veteran, thus depriving us of the pleasure of making snide remarks about home postings and the like!

We were issued with ' 'home posting" webbing gear, so had to re—acquaint ourselves with the twin curses of Blanco and Brasso, and pay a bit more attention to polishing our boots than we had become accustomed to. We also had our jungle green uniforms taken away and replaced by regulation battle dress and greatcoats. Our parkas had disappeared long ago. Now for the first time we could wear our medal ribbons — they were not worn when in "short sleeve order", nor on the jungle green jackets.

All Commonwealth Division personnel who had served a minimum of twenty four hours in Korea during the period of hostilities were awarded two campaign medals, the Korean War medal and the United Nations medal with a clasp reading "Korea." The UN medal was awarded to all in the UN forces. The medals themselves were not issued at this time, in fact I did not get mine until about four years later.

The Korean War ribbon was known colloquially as the "NAAFI Ribbon" for a rather convoluted reason. Instead of normal civilian-type number plates, it was the practice for all Army vehicles to have markings which identified the branch to which they belonged. Each branch had its own colours — for example, ours were red and blue. Identification was achieved by painting a square on the front and back of the vehicle in the owner's colours. On the squares was painted in white the vehicle's individual number, thus providing positive recognition of the vehicle and its owner.

On active service the duties performed by civilian staff in the NAAFI become the responsibility of the Royal Army Service Corps, whose colours happen to be yellow and blue, the same as on the medal ribbon — hence the nickname. There are five stripes on the ribbon, alternate yellow and blue, presumably representing the five Commonwealth nations with combat forces in Korea, i.e. Britain, Canada, Australia, New Zealand and South Africa.

The UN ribbon has seventeen narrow stripes in blue and white, in recognition I suppose of the sixteen members of the UN with forces there, plus South Korea itself. For rather more obvious reasons this ribbon was dubbed the "Butcher's Apron."

While at the Depot I was able to renew acquaintanceships with blokes I had not seen for eighteen months, and we had a good time swapping experiences over a few beers at the local pub. Some of them had been in Germany with the BAOR, and had some interesting yarns to tell. All in all our stay at Woolwich was pleasant enough, and passed quickly.

26

FREE AT LAST

At last the long-awaited Holy Grail of the National Serviceman was at hand — the fabled Early Breakfast! Those of us for whom the date of release was the 16th of September 1954 were now free of the administrative rigmarole of the discharge procedure. In those days the phenomenon of "counselling" was in its infancy — those about to leave the service received no advice that might have been useful in re- adjusting to civilian life. The only counsel that was offered to us was the stern admonition that we were in the Reserves for the next three and a half years, could be recalled to the colours at any time during that period, and were therefore not to change our address of record without notifying the authorities.

There were two forms of service in the Reserves — there was the Territorial Army and the Army Emergency Reserve. Reservists in the T.A. were obliged to attend a two-week training camp each year, as well as some weekend training sessions throughout the year, while the A.E.R. had only the two-week camp to contend with.

I was pleased to find that I was on the A.E.R. list — I attributed this stroke of good fortune to the fact that there was no Artillery T. A. regiment anywhere near my home, so that weekend training would be impractical because so much time would be lost in travelling. The only drawback was that I would have to take all my gear and keep it at home, whereas the T.A. people could leave most of their stuff at their depot.

After all the anticipation the Early Breakfast itself was a fairly low-key affair, and something of an anticlimax. All our goodbyes had been said at the farewell booze-up the night before, and many of us were feeling a bit fragile anyway. So after the meal we picked up our gear and our final pay, and went our separate ways.

Weighed down by all my military impedimenta, I arrived at Paddington Station and settled down on a bench, surrounded by my belongings, to wait for the next train for Cornwall, which was not due for another couple of hours. True to its traditions, the Army had supplied not only a free travel warrant, but also haversack rations, so with my water bottle filled, I was well provisioned for the journey, which I expected would take seven or eight hours. I still had a good supply of cigarettes, having stocked up before leaving the Dilwarra.

Despite the British reputation for reticence in the company of strangers, I had no trouble entering into conversation with my fellow passengers — no doubt my being in uniform helped to break the ice. It was music to my ears to hear the Cornish accent again, after being away for so long.

The journey was enjoyable — it was a bright, sunny day, and it was wonderful to soak up the ever-changing scenery as the train sped westward. As we crossed the Tamar into Cornwall, I swear the landscape was even more beautiful, and the grass greener! It was late afternoon by the time we reached Truro, where I had to change trains and catch the two-carriage local train for the last leg of my journey, the half-hour hop to Perranporth.

There was no one there to meet me, because being unsure of how good the train connections might be, I had not been able to tell my folks exactly when I would be arriving. By the time I had lugged all my baggage up the long hill to our home, I was just about all in, and after the greetings were over and I had had a good feed, I was glad to get to my bed! It was a strange feeling having a room to myself again there were a lot of things I would have to get used to.

My last pay totaled about seventy pounds, representing two years' savings plus the twenty two pounds I received for having been on active service, (known familiarly as the "Korea Bounty"), which was paid at the rate of ten pounds for the first three months or part thereof, and a pound a month after that. I had never before seen so much money at one time, but I was to find that it soon melted away. For one thing I had to spend a fair bit of it on new clothes, because all my old stuff was far too small for me now.

Unlike our predecessors, the veterans of the Second World War, National Servicemen did not receive a "demob suit" of civilian clothes. Obviously the Army didn't expect that we would outgrow our civvy gear in a mere two years, but I had grown about an inch and a half, and put on over a stone in weight since I joined up, so had nothing that would still fit. As a result I had to go about in uniform for a few days until I had bought some new gear.

27

THE AFTERMATH

In August of 1955 1 received orders to report for my first, and as it turned out, my only training camp with the A.E.R. I had been assigned to a field regiment which was based in Liverpool. The instructions were to join the regiment at Otterburn, a village in Northumberland close to the Scottish border, as far away from Cornwall as it was possible to get and still be in England.

On arrival after a long and tiring rail journey, I found that with the exception of two Welshmen, I was the only "foreigner" among a horde of Scouses. They were very clannish, and seemed to resent the intrusion of outsiders. Nor were the Taffies of much comfort — they both spoke Welsh as their preferred language, kept very much to themselves, and spoke to others only when it was unavoidable. It looked as though it was going to be a long fortnight!

It didn't worry me unduly though; I found it difficult in any case to take these war games seriously. What I found more disconcerting was the weather — I had left home at the height of summer, but in Otterburn it was more like midwinter. We were under canvas of course, and out on the barren moors the sea fog rolling in from the North Sea was bone-chilling, and this was August! It does not bear thinking about how it would have been to hold manoeuvres here in wintertime. There were sheep wandering around the campsite, and at night it was not unusual for a woolly head to poke itself through the tent flap and utter a mournful bleat.

Most days we were out on manoeuvres, setting up gun positions and loosing off a few rounds at an imaginary enemy. It passed the time, and at the weekend we were able to get into Otterburn, where I found the local people to be very friendly and hospitable. In the North they have institutions called "Working Men's Clubs" and I was invited to join the members as a guest on the Saturday night. I thoroughly enjoyed a great evening — a few games of darts and a sample of the excellent local brew in convivial company. They're grand lads, the Geordies.

I got into a bit of trouble at the end of one of the field exercises. As we were packing up after the manoeuvres, I asked the blokes who were already in the back of the three-tonner to give me a hand to load a chain into the truck. They refused, with some con-temptuous comment. I was not in a good mood anyway, being somewhat fed up with the whole business. So I snarled "Stand back", gathered up the chain and hurled it into the truck without further ado, causing the occupants to scatter.

The incident did nothing to improve my temper, and the situation deteriorated still further when the lance-bombardier of another squad raised a laugh by making some derogatory remark, accompanied by a smirk. I am not normally of a bellig-erent nature, preferring where possible to avoid confrontation, but this was the last straw. I challenged the NCO to take off his jacket (thus removing all sign of rank), and we would settle the matter. Fortunately he declined the offer, for I did not really want to fight, but anyway there was no more provocation.

It would be true to say that I gained very little pleasure out of the two week experience at Otterburn, and I was very glad to bid farewell to the Liverpool regiment and to the bleak moors of the border country — Cornwall had never seemed so inviting! In the event that was the last I saw of the regiment, and indeed of any sort of active involvement with the Army — probably the War Office had come to the conclusion that it wasn't worth the trouble and expense of bringing a handful of people from all over the country for such a futile exercise.

There were a few anxious moments in November 1956 though, when Anthony Eden foolishly decided to join France and Israel in the ill-advised invasion of the Suez Canal zone in an attempt to overthrow the Egyptian president Nasser after he had seized control of the Canal. Fortunately disaster was averted by the timely intervention of President Eisenhower, who put a speedy end to the folly. If the skirmish had escalated into widespread conflict, as seemed possible with the Russians making threatening noises, there might have been a need to recall some of the reservists.

The following year I went to live in Canada for a few years, and in early 1958 I received a letter from the War Office (forwarded by my parents, for I had neglected to advise the Army that I was no longer resident in the U K), requesting me to return my uniform and equipment, as my term in the Reserves had now expired. I was forced to confess that I was no longer in possession of these items, while not offering any information as to what had happened to them. I could hardly explain that I had given my greatcoat to my father to wear while driving the tractor in the winter, and that the hem of the coat had come into contact with the tractor exhaust and now had a hole in it. Or that my brother was using my small pack to carry his lunch to work, and it was by now beyond repair, having received fairly rough treatment. I had been using my uniform as work clothes, having removed all insignia, and consequently, like my boots, it was now far from being in parade condition. The rest of my gear had also disappeared, so offering a lame excuse, I diverted attention from the issue by politely requesting the authorities to forward my medals, which I had not yet received. They duly arrived a short time later with a brief formal note which made no further mention of the missing gear.

The Korean War medal deserves to be classed as a work of art. On one side is the image of the Queen and the inscription as on a coin, and on the other is a depiction of George and the Dragon, and the word KOREA. I thought the design was a stroke of genius, showing as it does St. George of Merrie England clobbering the evil Chinese Dragon! A veritable display of imagination, unusual in the Army. As a point of interest, it was the first campaign medal since the First World War to show the identity of the recipient — around the edge it is stamped with the person's number, rank, name and branch of service.

The UN medal is much more mundane — on one side is the UN emblem and a clasp reading KOREA, and on the other the sententious and rather clumsily-worded inscription: "FOR SERVICE IN DEFENCE OF THE PRINCIPLES OF THE CHARTER OF THE UNITED NATIONS." Phew!

I have kept these, as well as a few other bits and pieces — a pocket knife, a stainless steel shaving mirror, my passbook (AB 64 Pt. l), my cap badge, and a number of black and white photographs, most of them not very clear — all souvenirs of a period that was in many ways the most memorable of my life. Someone once said words to the effect that every man thinks better of himself for having been a soldier, and I believe that there may be some truth in the observation.

There is something about life in the Army that leaves a deep and abiding impression on those who have experienced it. It may be the living in close proximity with comrades who become like family, the shared trials and tribulations, the loss of freedom and individuality, and the interdependence of the group, that create a bond and camaraderie that cannot be duplicated in civilian life.

Although in all the years since my demob I have never come across any one of the scores of my former Army mates, I have spoken to many other ex-National Servicemen, and almost without exception their recollections of their Army days are positive.

The issue of National Service raises its head every so often in controversial discussions on whether or not its re-introduction would have any beneficial effects in combating teenage violence and crime, or the scourge of youth unemployment. I keep an open mind on the subject, not feeling competent to offer an opinion, and preferring to leave it to sociologists and others better qualified to judge. I can only say that from my perspective I really believe that it did me more "good than harm".

The End

U .N. ARMED FORCES IN KOREA

U.S.A.:
7 Army Divisions, I Marine Division, Army and Corps
Headquarters, Logistics and Support Troops, 1 Tactical Air Force,
I Combat Cargo Command, 2 Medium Bombardment Wings, & I
Complete Naval Fleet.

BRITAIN:
5 Infantry Battalions, 2 Field Regiments R.A., I Medium Battery
R.A., 1 Armoured Regiment, I Aircraft Carrier, 2 Cruisers, 8
Destroyers, with Marine and Support Units.

CANADA:
1 Army Brigade (3 Infantry Battalions, 1 Field Regiment R.C.A., 1
Armoured Regiment), 3 Destroyers, 1 Air Transport Squadron.

TURKEY:
1 Army Brigade (about 6000 men)

AUSTRALIA:
2 Infantry Battalions, 1 Fighter Squadron, 1 Air transport
Squadron, 1 Aircraft Carrier, 2 Destroyers, and 1 Frigate.

THAILAND:
1 Regimental Combat Team (4000 men), 2 Corvettes, 1 Air
Transport Squadron.

PHILLIPINES:
1 Regimental Combat Team.

FRANCE:
1 Infantry Battalion, 1 Gunboat.

GREECE:
1 Infantry Battalion, 1 Air Transport Squadron.

NEW ZEALAND:
1 Field Regiment R.NI.A.

NETHERLANDS:
1 Infantry Battalion, 1 Destroyer.

COLOMBIA:
1 Infantry Battalion, 1 Frigate.

BELGIUM:
1 Infantry Battalion

ETHIOPIA:
1 Infantry Battalion.

SOUTH AFRICA:
1 Fighter Squadron.

LUXEMBOURG:
1 Infantry Company.

Note: Other nations, e.g. Norway and India, contributed non-combatant personnel - medical units etc. The total U.S. contribution was about ten times the combined total of the other 15 nations.

www.ingramcontent.com/pod-product-compliance
Lightning Source LLC
Chambersburg PA
CBHW032057080426
42733CB00006B/305